NOTORIOUS AUSTRALIANS

NOTORIOUS AUSTRALIANS

the Mad, the Bad and the Dangerous

TOBY CRESWELL

ABC
Books

Published by ABC Books for the
AUSTRALIAN BROADCASTING CORPORATION
GPO BOX 9994 Sydney NSW 2001

Copyright © Toby Creswell

First published September 2008

All rights reserved. No part of this publication may be reproduced, stored in a retrieval system, or transmitted, in any form or by any means, electronic, mechanical, photocopying, recording or otherwise, without the prior written permission of the Australian Broadcasting Corporation.

National Library of Australia
Cataloguing in Publication entry

Creswell, Toby.
Notorious Australians.
ISBN 9780733317170 (pbk.).
1. Criminals – Australia – History. 2. Convicts – Australia – History. I. Australian Broadcasting Corporation. II. Title.
364.10994

Cover by Darian Causby/Highway 51
Typeset in 11.5/19pt Bembo by Kirby Jones

ABOUT THE AUTHOR

Toby Creswell has been writing about popular culture for some thirty years. He was the Editor of *Rolling Stone Australia* for eight years. In 1993 he became the editorial director of Terraplanet, a magazine and web publisher with titles including *Juice*, *HQ*, *Australian Style*, *monument*, *Big Hit*, *Esky*, *24hours* and many others. Terraplanet's magazines were awarded the highest professional commendations from the Magazine Publishers Association and the Society of Magazine Editors.

Toby has written a number of books including; *1001 Songs* (Hardie Grant), *Too Much Ain't Enough* (Random House), *Love is in the Air* (ABC Books), *1001 Australians* (with Samantha Trenoweth) (Pluto Press) and *The Real Thing* (with Martin Fabinyi) (Random House). He has been involved in writing documentaries for many years and his other television work includes live variety (as producer/writer) and event shows. He has been a commentator on cultural issues for ABC TV and Radio as well as Channel 4 and the BBC.

In 2007, Toby wrote and produced the series *Great Australian Albums* (Silverchair, Crowded House, the Triffids, the Saints) for

SBS. In 2008 he wrote and produced a second series of *Great Australian Albums* (Powderfinger, Nick Cave and the Bad Seeds, Hunters + Collectors, the Go-Betweens). Also in 2008, he has written and produced a documentary about the life of Johnny O'Keefe for ABC Television and *Cannot Buy My Soul*, a documentary on the singer and songwriter Kev Carmody.

CONTENTS

Introduction 1

The Mad

Richard Neville 7
Dawn Fraser 10
Dulcie Deamer 15
Errol Flynn 16
Felix the Cat 17
Frank Hardy 19
George Molnar 21
Sydney Sparkes Orr 24
Johnny O'Keefe 26
Lee Gordon 28
Les Darcy 30
Lola Montez 33

Norman Lindsay 35
Percy Grainger 37
Gary Ablett Senior 39
Samuel Marsden 42
Daniel Patrick Mannix 45
John Dowie 47
Charles Webster Leadbeater 48
William James Chidley 53
William Gocher 56
Leila Waddell 57
Rosaleen Norton 61
William Kamm 64

The Bad

General Count McHugo   71
John Dow   72
Lewis Lasseter   75
Roger Tichborne   78
The Fine Cotton Affair   82
Arthur Coningham   85
Peter Macari   90
John Stonehouse   91
Donald Cameron   94
The Weeping Woman   96
Wanda Koolmatrie   97
Elizabeth Kenny   100
Christopher Skase   103
Dr William McBride   107
Pemulwuy   111
Jundamurra   113
Mulla Abdulla   114

Henry James O'Farrell   117
Jessie Street   119
Jim Cairns   121
John Gorton   124
George Reid   127
Joh Bjelke-Petersen   128
John Kerr   133
Sir Robert Askin   135
Vladmir Petrov   136
Billy Wentworth   137
William Lane   140
William Hughes   142
Jack Lang   144
Eureka Stockade   148
The Battle of Vinegar Hill   151
Thomas Ley   154

The Dangerous

Alexander Pearce   161
The Gun Alley Murder   163
George 'Possum' Dean   165
Henry Bertrand   168
John Knatchbull   173
Jean Lee   175
Eugenia Falleni   178
Kevin Simmonds   179
Leonard 'Lennie' Lawson   181
Ronald Ryan   182
The Baby Farmers   184
Veronica Monty   187
The Family   189
The Snowtown Murders   192
Catherine and David Birnie   197
Eric Cooke   201
Dr Harry Bailey   204
Ivan Milat   208
Bradley John Murdoch   211
Paul Denyer/The Frankston Killer   212
William Blackstone   215
Crimes of Passion   216
Mount Rennie Outrage   218
Nellie Cameron   221
Kate Leigh   224
Tilly Devine   227
Thommos   231
Big Jim Anderson   232
Robert Trimbole   235
Nugan Hand Bank   238
Squizzy Taylor   241
Victor George Peirce/The Walsh Street Killings   244
Alphonse Gangitano   247
Mark 'Chopper' Read   249
Fred Cook   251
Dennis Allen   253
Graham 'The Munster' Kinniburgh   255
Raymond 'Chuck' Bennett   257
Ben Hall   258
Harry 'Breaker' Morant   259
Henry Redford   262
Jimmy Governor   263
Daniel 'Mad Dog' Morgan   265
Mary Ann Bugg   266
Ned Kelly   267

INTRODUCTION

As everybody knows, the British thought of Australia as an ideal place in which to deposit the scum of the earth. It's surprising then, that Australia has produced so few bad men and women.

Australians deeply cherish their convict heritage; indeed, what is known as the 'larrikin streak' could be interpreted as a diluted version of the convict strain. What follows here is a sample of notorious Australians, from the merely mischievous to the downright evil. These people have in some way contributed to what we know of the Australian character. Some of the bad behaviour could be put down to larrikinism; some of it, however, defies even the darkest parts of our history.

The larrikin tradition goes back to the First Fleet. The unhappy souls transported to the colony of New South Wales in 1788 were not the type to take the yoke of their penalty easily, but with little chance of escape they undertook small rebellions — signs of disrespect for authority, be that the church or the state.

Characters like the Reverend Samuel Marsden represent the colonial past — there was a man more wicked than the convicts to whom he was supposed to minister. Then there was Pemulwuy, an Aboriginal resistance fighter who was disinterested in the material advantages the British brought and just wanted them to go home — a view later adopted by most Australians. There were the hapless bank robbers and the rebel Phillip Cunningham, who led the battle of Vinegar Hill in the hope of bringing the Irish rebellion to Australia.

Fighting for Ireland in Australia was a venerable tradition upheld by Peter Lalor at the Eureka Stockade and Ned Kelly in his famous two-year stand against the troopers. It was a struggle carried into the second half of the twentieth century by Archbishop Daniel Mannix. This recalcitrant priest caused the British Navy to launch with the singular purpose of preventing him from arriving in Ireland.

Australia has always been a very secular nation. We have had our religious leaders but they have generally been more interested in politics than faith. We do have a strong line of unorthodox religious thinkers and one high priestess: Leila Waddell, who was the consort of the Great Beast, Aliester Crowley.

It has been suggested that Australians used to regard women as either damned whores or god's police; we have had more interesting women than either of those labels would imply. Lola Montez, while not Australian, shook the nation to its Victorian bootstraps with her spider dance while the witch of the Cross, Rosaleen Norton, cast spells that brought scandal to the highest reaches of society,

Introduction

Then there were the famous Sydney Queens, Kate Leigh and Tilly Devine, who were perhaps the toughest women gangsters of all time. They presided over the colourful years of the first half of the twentieth century — a time of sly grog, SP gambling, cocaine and vice. While these criminals were certainly tough people, Australian crime was an almost accepted part of society. The illegal casinos of Sydney entertained men from all walks of life. John Wren, who ran the famous Tote in Collingwood, was one of the most respected members of his community.

While a book on the history of crime in Australia is way too large a task for this modest volume, I have attempted to cover the main participants — the serial killers for whom we are internationally famous; the gangsters like Squizzy Taylor and the victims of being-in-the-wrong-place-at-the-wrong-time like Ronald Ryan and Jean Lee, or the Demon Dentist of Wynyard Square.

I have also covered some of the more colourful crime figures from the 1970s, such as Aussie Bob Trimbole and Frank Nugan, whose bank serviced both the CIA and the world's largest heroin empire at the same time.

It's worth noting that so many of Australia's early heroes were bushrangers who tended to hold up banks and rob from the rich — although they rarely gave to the poor. Ned Kelly, Mad Dog Morgan, Ben Hall: these are the archetypes of early Australia.

However, it's the larrikins who really won my heart. Richard Neville, for instance, was a nice middle-class boy who liked to cause trouble and in the process created two magazines, one of which caused him to wind up in an English jail, only to be sprung with the help of eminent QCs and John Lennon. Norman Lindsay delighted in provoking the god police, while Dawn Fraser was not only one of the world's greatest athletes but a woman who wouldn't be told. Errol Flynn put Tasmania on the map by living life too large.

We are a nation that has produced some spectacular imposters and frauds. Arthur Orton, the Tichbourne Claimant, drew most of Victorian London into his preposterous fantasy. And finally there are the politicians. No one exemplified the larrikin spirit better than Jack Lang, who stood up to the Bank of England, the Communists and the Australian Labor Party (ALP), earning the sobriquet 'Big Fella'. John Gorton was a man who wouldn't leave his mischievous side behind when he became prime minister, and in putting everyone's noses out of joint he helped to bring a sleepy nation into the modern world. There have been disasters — you couldn't find two more corrupt politicians than Joh Bjelke-Petersen or Robert Askin, except for Thomas Ley, the New South Wales Minister for Justice, who took to throwing his rivals off the cliffs at Coogee.

Most of these characters from our past were at least as sinned against as sinning. Some of them did it for love, some for money and many because they were just a little bit crazy. It's as true a cross-section of Australia as you're likely to find.

THE MAD — THE LARRIKINS AND ECCENTRICS

The proudest tradition in Australia is that of larrikinism. We are a nation that likes to see ourselves as thumbing our noses at authority, sticking pins in the self-important and questioning accepted wisdom — and doing it all with a sense of humour.

Richard Neville

Richard Neville was born in 1944 into the bosom of the bourgeoisie. He was educated at Knox Grammar, a private boys school on the upper north shore of Sydney. After matriculating he joined an advertising agency and later enrolled in an Arts Commerce degree course at the University of New South Wales. In 1961 Australia was a very uptight place. The Queen and Sir Robert Menzies loomed large in the national psyche; there was capital punishment, pubs closed at 6 p.m. and women stayed in the ladies' lounge; White Australia, cricket and the sheep's back were the pillars of the community. Dissent or satire — especially where these matters were concerned — was unthinkable.

At university Neville became involved in the student newspaper *Tharunka*, where as features editor he took it upon himself to shake things up. The first of many major media stunts was the kidnapping of Brian Henderson, then host of the pop music television program *Bandstand* (and later the most respected newsreader in the country, appearing on the Nine Network). 'Hendo' was captured by Neville and his accomplices, all dressed as beatniks, and held to a ransom of £100.

The following day *Tharunka* produced a parody of *The Sydney Morning Herald* newspaper that asserted that the Sydney Harbour Bridge was collapsing. They managed to hoax several thousand credulous Sydneysiders.

In March 1962 Neville became editor of *Tharunka* and formed a critical alliance with Martin Sharp, Australia's most brilliant pop artist. Across town, medical student Richard Walsh was the editor of Sydney University's *Honi Soit* newspaper. They teamed up and on April Fool's Day 1963 they published the first edition of *Oz*.

By issue three the editors had been served their first writs for publishing an obscene publication; in September that year they were found guilty and fined £20 each.

Oz was an amazing success. The magazine attracted a wide range of talent to its pages and an even wider range of controversy. The paper attacked every pillar of society, left no sacred cow unturned and satirised the suburban ocker unwashed.

A year after first publication, *Oz* was again charged with being an obscene publication. The defence team pulled out dozens of eminent thinkers to support the editors but it was to no avail: Neville and Walsh were sentenced to six months' hard labour and Sharp got three. Fortunately the conviction was overturned on appeal.

'When I produced *Oz*, legal action was the furthest thing from my mind,' Neville told George Negus. 'Mainly, I wanted to do a magazine that I could be proud of, and that my, you know, my peer group would be stimulated by. So, when — when the law started raiding newsagents and confiscating issues and burning them and a policewoman came to my home, no, I was really shocked and surprised, as indeed was my quite elderly father.

'We produced about twenty-six issues of *Oz* magazine in Australia, ... and our last big battle was about the Sydney Opera House. I knew nothing about opera, but we really understood that [Jorn] Utzon [the architect of the Sydney Opera House] was being crushed. So, we had this — yet another campaign to save something wonderful. I think that's one that *Oz* was on the right side of.'

The Oz Trials were major battles for the Left in Australia in the 1960s. At that time the censorship laws were strictly enforced and it took ten more years before a sensible balance was achieved. The notion of political satire and, indeed, a questioning of the traditional values of the Australian establishment were at that time just beginning. *Oz* took on issues that just weren't aired elsewhere, like the monarchy and the White Australia Policy.

Neville and Walsh then set sail for London, where they relaunched *Oz* with partners Felix Dennis and Jim Anderson. In London the stakes were even higher. A number of issues fell foul of the authorities and in 1971 the *Oz* editors —Neville, Anderson and Dennis — were charged with publishing obscenity and threatened with jail.

'When the *Oz* trials started, and they were reported by Fleet Street in, I think, pretty unfair terms, pretty sensationalist terms,' said Neville, 'I think people on the whole were against us. I mean, we represented long-haired, dope-smoking, anti-establishment wackos, and we were Australians to boot — at least, two of us were. But I think that after the judge sent us to jail before we were actually sentenced and ordered our hair to be cut, this wonderful kind of British sense of fair play came into motion and, almost overnight, they switched. And, suddenly, from being kind of deadbeat criminals, we became, you know, potential martyrs.'

A huge campaign was mounted. Eminent thinkers again came out in their favour; John Lennon organised a benefit single.

Richard Neville remained a voice of the counterculture through the 1970s.

He eventually returned to Australia, where he has continued to write. His book on the serial killer Charles Sobraj was a bestseller. He now calls himself a futurist.

Dawn Fraser

Few Australians have exemplified the Australian spirit as well as Dawn Fraser. She was born in 1937 in the Sydney suburb of

Balmain, then a blue-collar, no-nonsense waterside municipality populated by factory and waterside workers. At an early age Dawn was working for local SP bookmakers, running bets. She suffered with chronic asthma as a child and took up swimming to improve her lung capacity.

Almost as soon as she entered the water Fraser was marked for greatness. Her coach, Harry Gallagher, convinced Fraser to take swimming seriously and he trained her for five hours a day. Perhaps it was her Balmain background, but Fraser clashed with swimming authorities from an early age. When at the age of twelve she won a prize of two shillings at the local football club's annual picnic, she was classed as a professional and lost her amateur status for two years. This ridiculous exercise of authority was a harbinger of things to come.

However, Fraser's ambition would not be diminished by petty bureaucrats. When Gallagher moved to Adelaide, Fraser followed him. The hardships she went through in these years paid off in 1956, when she won gold in the 100 metres freestyle at the Melbourne Olympics. Two years later she took out two gold medals at the 1958 Commonwealth Games, and in 1960 she was the first woman to break one minute in the 100 metres freestyle. That year she also won Olympic gold in the 100 metres — which, in Balmain girl style, she celebrated by going out on the turps until the early hours of the morning. She woke to be told that she was swimming the butterfly leg of the relay that day. Fraser refused, just as she had refused to wear the team tracksuit. She was rewarded with another two-year ban.

The 1964 Tokyo Olympics were a triumph for Fraser and a nadir for officialdom. It looked as though Fraser might not go to Tokyo — during training she was seriously injured and her mother killed in the same car accident.

Grief stricken and confined by a back and neck brace, Fraser joined the Australian team anyway. Problems arose almost immediately: the swimming team manager refused to let Fraser march in the opening ceremony because her race was less than forty-eight hours away.

'I did go and speak to my team manager,' Fraser told the ABC Radio show 'The Sports Factor', 'and I said, "Look, I know I'm swimming thirty-seven hours after the opening ceremony, please let me march in the opening ceremony, it's something that puts the adrenalines into your body, it's the cream on the cake." And he said, "You are not marching." And I said, "But why? Why, Mr Slade, can't I march?" He said, "Because it'll hurt your legs." And I thought that was the poorest excuse, and I said to him, "Look, if I'm not fit enough to march around the arena in the opening ceremony of an Olympic Games with my Australian crest on my chest, I shouldn't be swimming. Because you're saying to me I'm not fit enough." Now I had worked very, very hard after the car accident in which my mother was killed to get to that Olympic Games, there was nothing, nothing that was going to stand in my way to winning a gold medal.

'I knew I had won the gold medal before I'd even swum in it, because I knew I was determined. And I knew because my times were faster than any other woman swimmer in the world. I was going into that race very egotistical, because they had to beat me and I knew that I was going to win that race. And I just felt it was a shame.

'I even went to the Chef de Mission and I said, "Look, Mr Kernow, can I march in the opening ceremony?" And he said, "Yes, have you got the uniform?" I said, "Yes I have, I've got everything with the exception of the gloves." He said, "Can you get the gloves?" I said, "Yes, Mrs Hatton's going to take me into Tokyo to get the gloves." He said, "I think you'd better get three other pairs too", that was for the other swimmers. Which I did.' Fraser marched.

Then came the next hurdle. Fraser disliked the team swimsuit — she thought it created too much drag — so she designed one of her own, which she insisted on wearing. 'I used to make my own swimsuits,' she told 'The Sports Factor'. 'I used to get the right material and make sure that I always had a special swimsuit, because I have got a long body and I always wanted to feel comfortable in my swimsuit. And especially when you've got to bend over and you've got officials standing behind you, there's nothing worse than to fall out of your swimsuit, and I was doing this.

'But also when I was diving in the water, I was going back to my early days of swimming, of my swimsuit filling up with water. And here I was in '64; we had progressed so greatly with materials of swimsuits. We'd gone from the wool to the silk to the nylon to the really nice material, and I'm still carrying an extra 5 pounds of water.'

Fraser's demands were justified when she won a third gold in the 100 metres — the first swimmer to win gold in the same event at three Olympic Games. And she won despite suffering an asthma attack that stopped her doing a tumble turn.

The Olympic triumph needed to be celebrated. One night in Tokyo, Fraser and three other team-mates swam the moat around the Imperial Palace and souvenired a Japanese flag. Fraser was a national hero to everyone except the officials in the swimming federation, who rewarded her record-breaking swimming with a ten-year ban, later reduced to four years. The ban effectively ended her sporting career. Despite the wrath of officialdom, Fraser was named Australian of the Year in 1964. Her final Olympic medal tally stood at four gold and four silver, and twenty-seven world records.

After quitting swimming, Fraser lived a rough-and-tumble life. She tried her hand at various business ventures including a cheese shop and, later, a pub in Balmain. She married and had a daughter but her married life was not smooth — she had a number of love affairs with both men and women.

In 1988 Dawn Fraser was elected to the NSW State Parliament to represent Balmain. Her life has been dedicated to her local community and, in outlook and character, she is the ultimate representation of that working-class suburb's larrikin spirit.

Proper recognition has come late in life: in 1999 the International Olympic Committee named Fraser the World Female Swimmer of the Century, and World's Greatest Living Female Water Sports Champion.

Dulcie Deamer

The woman dubbed the Queen of Bohemia was born Mary Elizabeth Kathleen Dulcie Deamer, the daughter of a physician, on 13 December 1890 in Christchurch, New Zealand. Dulcie Deamer made her first stage appearance at age nine and seemed set on a career on the stage. A short story published in the prestigious *Lone Hand* journal also led her into journalism and fiction writing.

By then resident in Australia, Dulcie joined a theatrical company and married Albert Goldberg (aka Goldie), the alcoholic father of her first child in 1908; he was almost twice her age. They had six more children. Deamer continued to perform on the stage, work for magazines and write journalism and novels. Her pulp fiction was widely admired in the United States, where it was syndicated and her novels published.

In 1922 Dulcie separated from Goldie. The children were billeted with their grandmother in Sydney, and Dulcie lived in Kings Cross among the artists, poets and dreamers of the time. The bohemians of Sydney had a big annual event, the Artists' Ball, and Deamer was the talk of the 1923 ball when she arrived in a caveman-like animal skin. Indeed, the outfit was the talk of Sydney for many years, and Dulcie's friends in the Roma café declared her the Queen of Bohemia.

In the 1930s Deamer wrote a number of well-regarded plays and continued writing journalism, often recording the Dionysian activities of her social milieu. She remained faithful to the Cross until her death there in 1972.

Errol Flynn

A descendent of a *Bounty* mutineer, Errol Flynn's life was as swashbuckling off screen as it was on. He was born at Hobart in 1909 to a marine biologist, Professor Theodore Thompson Flynn, and Lily Mary Young. He found trouble from an early age and was moved from a number of Hobart schools. He was then sent to Sydney Church of England Grammar School (Shore) but was expelled for bullying.

Honest work appealed to Flynn about as much as school had. He found his way to the New Guinea goldfields, where he later claimed to have traded slaves and searched for gold. In his autobiography, *My Wicked, Wicked Ways*, he boasted of seducing a woman and then robbing her of her jewellery. He also boasted of beating a Chinaman. This thief, racist and sexual predator was cast in Charles Chauvel's 1933 epic film *In the Wake of the Bounty*. He had found his destiny.

Flynn moved to England, where he pursued an acting career. Chauvel's film led to him securing the lead in *Captain Blood*. His next film, *The Adventures of Robin Hood*, made him a star and he went on to appear in almost sixty films. His major successes were *The Charge of the Light Brigade* (1935), *The Private Lives of Elizabeth and Essex* (1939), *They Died With Their Boots On* (1941) and *The Adventures of Don Juan* (1948).

Off screen Flynn was legendary for his sexual prowess and wild behaviour. His first marriage to screen temptress Lili Damita was notorious for its scenes of drunkenness and violence. Flynn was a keen user of morphine and other drugs, and was known to host sex parties with both men and women.

Flynn was charged with statutory rape in 1942, although he was acquitted. By the 1950s, he was washed up. An alcoholic, he stumbled through marriages and more rape charges. His last romantic involvement was with fourteen-year old Beverly Aadland, whom he planned to marry, but he died of a heart attack in 1959, survived by four children. Flynn's eldest son, Sean, became an acclaimed photojournalist. He disappeared in the Cambodian jungle, where he was executed by the Khmer Rouge in 1971.

Felix the Cat

Felix the Cat — the wonderful, wonderful cat — had his origins in the small Sydney newspapers where Pat Sullivan developed his flair for cartooning. Born on 22 February 1885 at Ivy Street, Paddington, Sullivan worked at Tooth's brewery while developing his penmanship. In 1909 he sailed for London, where he continued to draw but found work hard to come by; he took other employment on the music-hall stage and as an animal handler. In 1910 he was in New York, boxing for a living.

Sullivan found cartooning easier in America and he worked on several syndicated newspaper comic strips, gradually moving into animation. Working in a number of studios, Sullivan turned out cartoon characters and a series based on Charlie Chaplin.

In 1917 Sullivan was jailed for nine months on a rape charge. While on bail he married Marjorie Gallagher and after his release they formed an animation studio. Their first film was *The Tail of Thomas Kat* (1917), followed two years later by *Feline Follies* (1919). Sullivan's studio took off and the demand for Felix pictures escalated. Sullivan assigned Otto Messmer to draw the cat, whose name was changed from Thomas to Felix in 1920 at the suggestion of a distributor.

In the early 1920s Felix the Cat was one of the largest stars in cinema. There were Felix shorts released every fortnight and his star power rivalled Chaplin and many of the actors of the period. The cartoons were aimed at an adult audience and dealt with issues ranging from prohibition and communism to Cubism and surrealist art movements. Sullivan was one of the first to realise the licensing opportunities offered by Felix and let his image be used on all manner of household goods. He was a fierce protector of his copyright and when a young animator, Walt Disney, devised a cat called Julius, Sullivan sued him and stopped the use of the character.

Disney was to have the last laugh, however. Sullivan resisted the arrival of sound after the 1928 release of Disney's *Steamboat Willie*, which starred Mickey Mouse. That film changed animation history and the mouse supplanted the cat. By that stage there had been 100 Felix films; the aviator Charles Lindbergh had even taken a Felix doll with him on his historic flight across the Atlantic Ocean. Felix had led the 1927 Thanksgiving Parade in New York and was already the only star on television. RCA used a Felix doll on a turntable to film its test broadcasts as they developed television technology. The tests continued until 1931.

By then, though, Sullivan was in trouble. His transition to sound had been a failure. He succumbed to syphilis and chronic alcoholism, and when his wife died in 1932 he completely fell to pieces. The studio collapsed and Sullivan died in 1933.

Otto Messmer continued drawing Felix for the next thirty years for comic strips and film, but the character never regained its earlier popularity. Claims have been made that Messmer was the original author of Felix but these have not been sustained.

Frank Hardy

One of Australia's best-known communists, Frank Hardy, was born in 1917 at Bacchus Marsh in Victoria. His family was working-class Catholic and he left school at thirteen to undertake a variety of menial jobs. Hardy was posted to Darwin in the Second World War and it was here that he began seriously writing journalism. He continued in the trade after the war

Hardy soon turned his attentions to fiction. In 1950 he self-published his epic masterpiece *Power Without Glory*. The novel's protagonist, John West, was based in part on Melbourne gangster and businessman John Wren. Hardy believed that Wren had sold out his working-class roots and was now a predator on the proletariat who exercised power through his relationships with the church and the ALP.

Hardy sold the book on street corners, in pubs and at community and political meetings. Unlike most self-published books, however, *Power Without Glory* was really good. Both the book and Hardy became a great success. Then Prime Minister Robert Menzies passed the *Communist Party Dissolution Act* and three days later Hardy was arrested for criminal libel. It was alleged that the book libelled Wren's wife with the allegation that Nellie West (the Ellen Wren character) was an adulteress, and Menzies was keen to prosecute communists. Hardy won the case — the book benefitted from the publicity.

Hardy remained a communist even after most members deserted the party in the late 1950s, with some consequences, although his political activism also brought results. The ABC's managing director of the time unsuccessfully pressured the broadcaster to shun Hardy. The Literature Board declined a grant to him of $3000 on the grounds of his politics — this led then Prime Minister Gough Whitlam to establish the Australia Council for the Arts, a body supposedly free of direct political control. Hardy and Nugget Coombs lobbied Whitlam on behalf of the Gurindji people, and this led to a major land rights initiative from Whitlam.

Hardy continued to write novels such as *But the Dead Are Many: A Novel in Fugue Form* and *Outcasts of Foolgarah*. He was popular on television and as a political commentator right up to his death in 1994. A 1999 poll in the *Sydney Morning Herald* and *The Age* voted

Power Without Glory the most influential work of Australian fiction in the twentieth century.

George Molnar

The elder George Molnar was a cartoonist and architect; the other was an anarchist and philosopher, a leading figure in the Sydney Push in the 1960s and '70s. George Molnar the younger was born in Budapest in 1934. His father escaped Hitler in the company of his secretary, leaving Molnar and his mother to their own devices to avoid the Holocaust and the refugee camps and make their way to Sydney, arriving in 1951. Molnar read economics and philosophy at Sydney under John Anderson and enthusiastically embraced Anderson's Libertarian movement of free thoughts and free love.

The Libertarian Society was formed as a de facto extension of Sydney University's Philosophy Department in the mid-1950s. Molnar was one of its leading members. He was gifted with a great mind but had one drawback as a member of the Push: he couldn't hold his liquor and preferred a coffee house as a venue for his pontifications. As a bohemian he drove taxis and believed in his own gambling systems, backing an entire year's wages on a poker game. Unfortunately, he was a terrible gambler.

Libertarianism saw itself as an opposition to authority and to moralism, especially in issues of relations between adults. The society published intellectually rigorous papers but was also known for frequenting the waterfront and trade union pubs, where issues were vigorously debated and undergraduate women seduced.

Outside the university they were known as the Push. Barry Humphries famously described them as 'a fraternity of middle-class desperates, journalists, drop-out academics, gamblers and *poets manqués*, and their doxies'.

An agent from ASIO was more kind, noting in 1959: 'At first meeting with these people one is inclined to regard them as an offshoot of the "beatniks", but after knowing them a short while it becomes obvious that they are well above the average "beatnik" intellectually. Their knowledge of Marxism is surprising and their ability to discuss this subject on levels not encountered in the Communist Party of Australia is both stimulating and educational.

'With the exception of Jim Baker, the Libertarians have absolutely no standard of ethics. Their behaviour and conversation in mixed company would be regarded as "shocking" even in "modern" society.

'They have no respect for property and live entirely within their own periphery of standards, which can only be described as obscure … The Libertarians should not be underestimated despite their base outlook.'

Free love probably had the edge over free thought in attracting Push members. One pharmacy student recalled an evening in 1962 when he ventured to the Royal George Hotel in Sydney: 'I spoke to no-one all evening and no-one spoke to me until just before closing time when I went outside … and two policemen seized

The Mad — The Larrikins and Eccentrics

me. I was flung into the back of a Black Maria and driven to the back of Darling Harbour ... They tipped me out into the cold night air and gave me a lecture: "Look, son, don't you go near that pub again — it's full of loose women, social diseases and drugs." I thought "Terrific!" and was back there next night.'

What had started as a philosophical salon became the subject of tabloid fascination. The attention of the yellow press intensified after the deaths of Gilbert Bogle and Margaret Chandler on New Year's Eve 1962.

The Bogles and the Chandlers were on the periphery of the Push. Gilbert Bogle was a CSIRO scientist about to move to move to the US. Margaret Chandler's husband, Geoffrey, was a Push fellow traveller and left his wife in Bogle's care while he pursued an affair of his own across town.

On New Year's morning Mr Bogle and Mrs Chandler were found semi-naked in the bush on the banks of the Lane Cove River with no apparent cause of death. There was a popular view for a time that they had taken LSD. This explanation fitted in well with the popular image of free love and drug taking and it all seemed very exotic. The fact there have been no other LSD overdoses in forty years hasn't diminished the popularity of this theory. It seems more likely, in fact, that another woman at the party who had been having an affair with Bogle and was very jealous killed the pair. The police were never able to get enough evidence to charge her. Nonetheless, the idea of the Push was now fixed in the public mind. Consequently the Push faded.

Molnar remained a leading figure in the Left as the Sydney bohemians moved from discussions in the Royal George to political activism against the Vietnam War and censorship.

An illegal raid on Molnar's house led to the creation of the Council of Civil Liberties. In the 1970s he contributed to Wendy Bacon's tenure as editor of NSW University's paper, *Tharunka*, and its sequel, *Thorunka* — both of which found themselves before the courts in the last great Australian censorship battle of the twentieth century.

Molnar gradually withdrew from both philosophy and politics for the 1980s and most of the following decade. He moved to England, where he became radical Left activist, and then returned to Australia, where he climbed the ladder of the Department of Veterans' Affairs before finally returning to academia shortly before his death. He was widely regarded as one of the better minds in the field but never finished his major work. He died in 1999, at age sixty-five, on the steps of Fisher Library at Sydney University after suffering a massive heart attack.

Sydney Sparkes Orr

Australia's greatest academic scandal broke in 1956, when the chair of the Philosophy Department at the University of Tasmania was dismissed for conducting an extramarital affair with an eighteen-year-old student

The Mad — The Larrikins and Eccentrics

Sydney Sparkes Orr was born in Northern Ireland in 1914. He had a reputation as an eccentric thinker and good teacher at the time he took up a position at Melbourne University. While waiting for his wife, Sadie, to join him he began an affair with a student. When Sadie arrived from England she was moved in with Orr's lover. The ménage broke up when the young woman became pregnant to the professor and returned, with the child, to her family in Sydney.

Orr was recommended for the newly established chair in Philosophy at the University of Tasmania in 1952. It's likely that the Melbourne faculty wanted to get rid of him as he was scandal prone and ill disciplined. Things went well in Hobart for a time. Orr was known to be lecherous towards his students but was well enough liked. He became very involved in the administration of the university and made serious criticisms of the way the university was run. His complaints, with others', were responsible for the establishment of a royal commission into the university in 1955.

Orr began an affair with one student, Suzanne Kemp. It was her first relationship and she was deeply affected by Orr. However, she ended the affair within six months. Her father discovered what had been going on and made a complaint to the university.

At first Orr denied the allegations. It was not uncommon at the time for academics to have affairs with their pupils and Orr's denial was regarded with some scepticism, especially given his past form. Nonetheless, Orr claimed that Suzanne was psychologically unbalanced and that the charges were motivated by the university administration as payback for the royal commission.

Orr was dismissed; the Australian academic world stood behind him. Academics were forced into the position of defending academic freedom and reluctantly adopted the Orr case. The Philosophy chair at Hobart was black-banned and Orr became a cause célèbre. Orr issued writs of libel against the university and fought for six years. He declined to settle the case, thus forcing his own family into poverty, until just before his death in 1966.

When not complaining about persecution, Orr maintained that he was the bastard son of King Edward VIII, which led to the verse 'A lunatic prof named Orr':

Declared his own mother a whore
From the fantastic themes
Of his Freudian dreams
He deduced that his père was a Windsor.

Johnny O'Keefe

Johnny O'Keefe was the king of Australian rock'n'roll. Born into a middle-class Sydney family in 1935, Johnny enrolled to study economics at Sydney University and worked in the family business, R M O'Keefe & Co. — but selling furniture was not for him. At night he was imitating American pop singer Johnny Ray in cabarets.

In 1955 Johnny saw the film, *Blackboard Jungle*, and, like thousands of young people around the world, was galvanised by its theme song, Bill Haley's 'Rock Around the Clock'. O'Keefe switched to rock'n'roll and toughened up his act. Two years later when Bill Haley toured Australia, O'Keefe befriended him. Haley gave O'Keefe a song, 'You Hit the Wrong Note, Billy Goat', and O'Keefe used his unstoppable promotional skills to parlay that association into a contract with Festival Records. 'Billy Goat' was issued — on 45 rpm and 78 rpm discs — in July 1957 and was arguably the beginning of Australian rock'n'roll.

O'Keefe cultivated promoter Lee Gordon and was soon appearing on the bill with international touring acts like Little Richard. Gordon and O'Keefe set up the Leedon label together and O'Keefe also started his own circuit of rock'n'roll dances around Sydney. In 1958 he co-wrote 'The Wild One' — also known as 'Real Wild Child' — which was the first locally written rock'n'roll hit. He was the first Australian rock'n'roll star to crack the Top 40. Overseas, Jerry Lee Lewis and Little Richard covered 'The Wild One' (more recently it has been covered by Iggy Pop).

In 1959 O'Keefe was the star of the ABC TV show *Six O'Clock Rock*; that same year he signed with Liberty Records in the US. The following year he toured the US promoting 'She's My Baby' and 'It's Too Late'. The latter song made number 1 in New York and New Orleans but failed to impress much beyond that.

O'Keefe returned to Australia, bought a large car and embarked on a massive national tour. On 27 June 1959 O'Keefe's Plymouth Belvedere ran off the road outside Kempsey, New South Wales. He received sixty-four stitches in his head and another twenty-six in his hands; he never fully recovered. He went back to *Six O'Clock Rock* but a year later transferred to Channel Seven in a show that was later renamed *Sing Sing Sing*. For the next three years O'Keefe maintained his cracking pace of recording, touring, artist management, record production and TV appearances. However, he was now the victim of regular mood swings and frequent breakdowns.

In 1964 the Beatles finally conquered Australia and the careers of the previous generation of performers were reallocated to the leagues clubs. But O'Keefe stuck at it. In the early 1970s he rode the wave of a '50s revival back into the limelight. By the time of his death from barbiturate poisoning in 1978, he had twenty-nine Top 40 hits to his name. A successful musical, *Shout!*, was based on his life story

Lee Gordon

Born in Detroit, Michigan in 1923, Lee Gordon had made and lost a fortune in electrical retailing by the time he arrived in Australia in 1953. Like his future friend Johnny O'Keefe, he initially sold furniture. He saw an opportunity to bring American entertainers to Australia and in 1955 presented Frank Sinatra at the Sydney Stadium. Other tours followed — notably one by Johnny Ray, who was washed up in the US. Gordon brought him to Australia and marketed the show into a massive success. Gordon also toured many of the jazz greats of the time. 'We started in July '54. We were over a million quid in front by March 1955. By August 1955 we were broke,' recalled Gordon's accountant, Alan Heffernan. 'One time we owed Pan Am $30 000. So we went to America. Pan Am had their head office in San Francisco and the woman at the counter said, "What do you want?" and Lee said, "We've come to have a meeting with your general manager about owing you people $30 000." So a guy came out to the counter and Lee said, "I'm Lee Gordon and this is Alan Heffernan, my associate. We owe you a lot of money. We want a meeting to see if we can solve the problem." They had their board there all lined up. I explained to them that the money was not owing by Lee Gordon or by Lee Gordon Big Shows, it was owing by Big Shows Pty Limited, which was a proprietary company and had no money and would go into liquidation. Lee said if you will back us on a return show of Nat King Cole and a third show on Johnny Ray, we'll make enough to pay you what we owe you, plus what we're going to owe you. Lee said, "I'll give you my personal guarantee." This was Lee's crowning stroke — "I'll give you my personal guarantee". It wasn't worth two bob. But it gave them a way out. They accepted his personal guarantee, arranged to give us the seating to bring down Nat King Cole in the following January and Johnny Ray in the February and carry over what we owed them.'

In 1957 Lee Gordon brought Bill Haley and the Comets to Australia and began a series of promotions that would see most of the international music stars appear in Australia. Gordon was no stranger to amphetamines and other drugs, and was subject to major mood swings. He made and lost several fortunes. But he was a hipster at heart. In 1962 he toured controversial American comic

Lenny Bruce, who was also a pethidine addict. The tour lasted one show in Sydney before it was closed on the basis of obscenity and Bruce was run out of town.

'Lenny Bruce was right off his head and Lee was very, very far out at that time,' Heffernan recalled. 'And nowadays, thinking back on it, it was his last gesture. He knew he was finished in Australia and he thought, "I'll go out on flame-blasting thing by bringing this act that will never be accepted in Australia."'

As well as promoting entertainers, Gordon started drive-in restaurants, American wrestling and a roller derby. He also created the first all-male revue, which became Les Girls.

In January 1962 in Acapulco, Mexico, Gordon married Arlene Topfer, a Queensland-born dancer and model, with Frank Sinatra as best man. A year later he was busted for possession of pethidine. Shortly after his arrest he left for London, where he died in November of that year. His son was born the following year.

Lee Gordon's mercurial, maverick career shook up Australia and blew out the colonial cobwebs forever.

Les Darcy

James Leslie Darcy was born in 1895, one of ten children, in a bark hut in Maitland, in the NSW Hunter region. His father was a sharecropper and farm labourer. From the age of fourteen, Darcy showed a talent for boxing. His strength was greatly improved after

The Mad — The Larrikins and Eccentrics

he was apprenticed as a blacksmith, and by fifteen he was fighting in tournaments and had earned the name 'The Maitland Wonder'.

Darcy moved to Sydney to fight for promoter Snowy Baker at the Sydney Stadium. When a controversial decision went against Darcy in his first fight, against American middleweight Fritz Holland, the outraged punters burned the shed to the ground.

At that time Sydney was a major port on the boxing circuit and Darcy faced the best American middleweight fighters of his age. In his first bout with American Jeff Smith he complained of a low blow in the fifth round. The referee thought he was shirking and gave the fight to Smith. But in a rematch Smith's blow to the groin saw justice restored. In one match Darcy lost his two front teeth. They were stapled back into his face with gold pins and the fight continued.

At just nineteen years of age Darcy was middle- and heavyweight boxing champion of Australia, and a contender for the world crown. In all he won forty-six out of his first fifty fights. In 1916 Darcy KO'd Harold Hardwick to capture the Australian heavyweight title. He was by then the most popular sportsman in Australia and a genuine working-class hero. Glory was not his motivation, though: Darcy's major interest in boxing was to send money back to his mother in Maitland.

Darcy had intended to enlist in the First Australian Imperial Forces as soon was war was declared in 1914. However, as he was underage, Darcy needed his mother's permission to enlist. She refused. Whether she was worried that he might die on the battlefield or whether, as a good Irish Catholic, she supported

Archbishop Mannix's opposition to World War I is unclear. Regardless, Darcy was branded a coward. He received white feathers in the mail. His titles were stripped from him and he was unable to get a bout in Australia.

In October 1916, shortly before his twenty-first birthday, Darcy stowed away on the *SS Cushing* bound for the US. Newsreels had carried footage of his fights to the US and he was already a hot property there. He had a shot at the world title. Denied a passport, he boarded the ship at Newcastle and hid under a tarpaulin.

Unfortunately for Darcy, by 1916 America was on the verge of entering the war. There was another outcry branding him a coward for leaving his country. Journalist Damon Runyon wrote, 'The commercial eye of the fight promoters recognised his money-making possibilities and they caused him to forget his duty.' His American tour fell apart. But Darcy became an American citizen and enlisted in the army.

As he was completing his army training and simultaneously his boxing training, in the hope of getting his career back on track, he developed blood poisoning as a consequence of the gold staples in his mouth. Pneumonia followed. He died in Memphis, Tennessee, at age twenty-one, on 24 May 1917.

In death, all was forgiven. Between a quarter and half a million people lined the streets of Sydney when his coffin passed through on its way to Maitland.

'The whole story of Les Darcy is really the story of a boy's love for his mother,' said family friend Harry Boyle. 'And he done everything for her, like, to put her on easy street. And it was her, actually, by refusing to sign his enlistment papers and that, that caused all his trouble.'

Lola Montez

Lola Montez was the most infamous dancer of the nineteenth century. Born in Ireland in 1821 as Dolores Eliza Gilbert, she was raised in India. She eventually married a young British officer and lived for a time there. After she caught her husband philandering, Montez left him. She then embarked on a successful career as a courtesan with, among many others, the composer Franz List and King Ludwig I of Bavaria, who had already grown mad and made her Baroness Rosenthal and Countess of Lansfeld. In return she was credited with hastening the hapless king's downfall.

In need of a career, Montez became a dancer, freely adapting her vision of the Spanish dance 'La Tarantula' which she was known to perform 'innocent of lingerie'. Also known as the Spider Dance, La Tarantula was based around a narrative of a young woman attacked by large spiders, and her dance is based on her movements to get the creatures off her. It has a certain element of horror and of panic and was strangely erotic, especially when interpreted by Lola.

According to one report, 'As the dance grew more frantic she shed the spiders and stamped then underfoot. They were stage props made of whalebone, cork or rubber. When the music changed to a jig Lola spread out her hands and feet like a spider and leaped from one side of the stage to the other. The effect was as grotesque as it was riveting.'

Having scandalised Europe, Montez arrived in New York in 1851. Her performance on Broadway was described as 'a certain routine of steps, without regard to time, music or anything else'. But Montez was the most modern of entertainers. A century and half later we are deluged by celebrities who are known for nothing more than their sexual prowess and for whom thousands will turn out just to see the seductress. As with Anna Nicole Smith and Paris Hilton, so too was it with Lola Montez.

Montez took her artistry seriously enough to raise her horsewhip at critics, as she would in Australia.

Baroness Montez and her manager, Noel Follin — who had left his wife and children to take up his post — arrived in Australia in 1855. Her visit started well enough when the *Waratah* berthed in Sydney and the police arrived to arrest her for nonpayment of her debts. She allegedly stripped naked and challenged the modest officers to arrest her.

The Sydney establishment abhorred her, as did Melbourne, and Geelong refused her permission to perform at all. Montez had had some success in the Californian gold rush and visited Ballarat, where the miners greeted her enthusiastically. They were known to shower the stage (lightly) with gold nuggets.

As usual, Montez had her problems with the press — specifically, with Harry Seekamp, editor of the *Ballarat Times*. She had debauched with the editor who then turned on her and said he would drive her off the diggings in print. Montez's response was to get out her whip and threaten to use it on the hypocrite.

Lola also threatened the manageress of the Ballarat theatre, who responded by beating Montez in a fight. Nonetheless, Montez's fame spread across Australia. Her Tarantula was considered the most erotic thing to happen to the colonies in a century, to say nothing of her approach to sleazy journalists. Montez departed Australia in 1856 as an even greater star than she had been when she arrived.

News of Montez's scandalous Australian tour spread to the rest of the world and added to her infamy. She returned to America and took up the pen, writing such books as *Anecdotes of Love: Being a True Account of the Most Remarkable Events Connected with the History of Love; in All Ages and among All Nations* (1858), *The Arts of Beauty, or, Secrets of a Lady's Toilet with Hints to Gentlemen on the Art of Fascination* (1858), and *Lectures of Lola Montez, Including Her Autobiography* (1858).

Lola Montez died of pneumonia in New York in the winter of 1861.

Norman Lindsay

A childhood visit to the Ballarat Art Galley introduced Norman Lindsay to J Solomon's *Ajax and Cassandra*, an historical and rather overblown study of passion that set Lindsay on his course.

Born in 1879 at Creswick, Victoria, Lindsay showed an early gift for draftsmanship and illustration. He and his brother Lionel began working for magazines in Melbourne; in 1901 they joined the staff of *The Bulletin* and Norman turned out illustrations and cartoons. His irreverent humour, racism and interest in Australian culture fitted in well with the magazine.

Lindsay also wrote. Perhaps his best-known work is *The Magic Pudding* (1917) but there were others such as *Redheap* (1930), *Saturdee* (1933) and *The Age of Consent* (1935). *Redheap* was banned for its overt discussion of sex.

As a painter, Lindsay was a very good cartoonist — however, his paintings are what made his name. He specialised in soft-porn pictures of voluptuous women cavorting nakedly in neoclassical scenes. The pictures shocked polite society but were hung in some of the most famous bars of Sydney and were quite in demand.

'When they're massed together like enormous gladioli, as here in the old man's house at Springwood, the effect is quite overpowering,' art critic Robert Hughes told the ABC. 'But what overpowers you is not so much their sexual content as their unique combination of vulgarity and innocence.'

Lindsay caused further scandal when he left his first wife for one of his models, Rose Soady. While they were unconventional people, they lived modestly together in Springwood in the NSW Blue Mountains for ten years and had three children out of wedlock.

'Now, bawdy is entirely different to pornography,' said Lindsay once. 'Bawdiness is a condition of life. Mankind spends his life retaining bawdy stories. Everything I did was "indecent". I was "a monstrous fellow". I was out to "violate all popular morality" and everything else. I wasn't doing anything of the sort. I cared for nothing but to express myself.'

Norman Lindsay died at Springwood in 1969.

Percy Grainger

Percy Grainger ranks among the greats of twentieth-century music, but is just as widely remembered for his eccentric behaviour. The only son of John, a talented but alcoholic architect, and Rose, a possessive mother, George Percy Grainger was born at Brighton in Melbourne on 8 July 1882. Rose was greatly disturbed by the fact that her husband had given her syphilis and the parents parted when Percy was eleven.

Rose doted on her son and encouraged his piano playing to the point where by the age of ten he was giving recitals in Melbourne. In 1899 she took her son to Europe to further his education in music. As a teen, Percy had progressed to giving concerts. Perhaps his natural boyishness led to his showmanship. He was known for pausing in a concert to tell jokes; in later years he would push the piano around the stage as he was playing. He often walked to concerts over distances of some miles and then strode into the concert hall and walked directly onto the stage. Despite his unconventional habits, he was well regarded by his contemporaries such as Edvard Grieg.

Grainger developed an interest in traditional folk music and was determined to preserve these ancient songs before they disappeared. One of his most popular adaptations of English folk music was 'Country Gardens', which is still often played today.

In 1914 Grainger moved to America, where his tours were even more popular than in Europe. When he married his mistress, Ella Viola Strom, in 1928 he did it at the Hollywood Bowl in front of 20 000 fans.

In America Grainger's music took a more experimental turn. He began designing his own instruments and experiment with new tonalities. One famous piece, 'The Warriors', was performed in Chicago with nineteen pianos and a percussion section.

Grainger held many peculiar ideas. He was a white supremacist who believed that the Scandinavians and English were the most pure of human races; not surprisingly, he found sympathy with Nazism. He deplored the way that English had been modified by other languages and invented his own vocabulary of words that had strictly Anglo-Saxon derivatives in them — a restaurant was an 'eat shop'. He was inclined to odd diets, wearing shorts made from towelling and to walking — sometimes up to 65 miles at a time. He was disinclined to wash his clothes. He had little interest in money and when he became wealthy from his concerts he gave much of it away, often to homeless people he met in the street or to young struggling musicians. He preferred to stay in cheap accommodation rather than the lavish hotels he could afford.

Grainger was always close to his mother, to a degree that seemed inappropriate. This closeness and Grainger's other habits led to rumours of an incestuous relationship between the two. There is, however, no evidence to support this theory. In any case, the stigma plagued Rose, who also suffered encroaching insanity from the syphilis. In 1932 she committed suicide by jumping from a New York hotel window.

Grainger's most notorious habit and joy, however, was flagellation. He took to it early in life and it became one of the factors that shaped his personality. Like many fetishists, Grainger ascribed spiritual aspects to the practice. 'I attach enormous importance to flagelantism,' he wrote. 'It is a means of turning the hostile, harsh and destructive elements in a man into harmless channels.' He lost more than a few lovers through his insistence on the whip, until he met Ella Viola Strom, who was prepared to put up with the pain.

Grainger became an American citizen but never forgot his roots. He established a trust, and after his death in 1961 a Percy Grainger museum was established in Melbourne to house his whips and his music, his suits and his unique instruments.

Gary Ablett Senior

Fame can do terrible things to a man, and no star has had a more tragic fall that Gary Ablett, Sr, the genius footballer from Geelong in Victoria was known as 'God'.

Born in 1961, Ablett played 248 first-grade games, mostly wearing the number 5 shirt for Geelong Football Club. The full forward scored more than 1000 goals before his retirement in 1997, but unfortunately his career will be forever overshadowed by his troubled personal life. He was never quite able to cope with fame and turned at one time to fundamentalist Christianity and at another to hard drugs.

'By any definition, Gary Ablett is a football genius,' said commentator Ron Evans. 'A football genius who has always been a troubled soul.'

'He was a freak,' added his manager, Michael Baker, of Ablett's abilities on the field. 'A freak that comes along not just once in every generation but once in every five generations, I think.'

Like any sports hero, Ablett attracted fans; one of them was twenty-year-old Alicia Horan. The pair had an affair in February 2000, which culminated in a five-day drug and alcohol binge in the Park Hyatt Hotel in Melbourne and the death of Horan.

Ablett had been depressed following the end of his career; he was using large amounts of heroin and ecstasy to deal with his emotional problems. He was also sharing the drugs. The coronial inquiry into Horan's death found that Ablett should have exercised more judgement given the youth and vulnerability of his companion.

Detective Senior Constable Nairn, the officer who charged Ablett, said that '[Horan's] infatuation with Mr Ablett caused her to ignore any inhibitions she may have had' about drug taking.

The Mad — The Larrikins and Eccentrics

Ablett was clearly out of control himself and probably only survived the drug orgy because of a stronger constitution and a higher tolerance. In the end He surrendered to police but it was all too little and too late.

Ablett was deeply disturbed by Horan's death. In its wake he declined the invitation to join the AFL's Hall of Fame but was inducted anyway. He did not attend the ceremony.

Australians are not, by and large, god-fearing. While our cousins in the United Kingdom and the United States have long and deep religious traditions, Australia has had a more materialistic culture. The British and, particularly, the Americans had theologians starting their own faiths in response to the new land and to new cultures; the Australians were more practical. Perhaps as with most things in Australia, this can be explained by the settlement of the country by outlaws and misfits.

Certainly there was a strong Protestant work ethic in the original settlement of the colony. The promoters of the Australian experiment in London hoped that transportation would be good for the soul, but it was difficult to arrange.

There were few men of the cloth enthusiastic enough to make the trip and many of those who did soon gave up hope of making much of an impression and threw themselves into the opportunities to acquire wealth alongside the other settlers. Some of them also became great Australian characters.

Samuel Marsden

Samuel Marsden was the first man of the church to make a great impression on Australia. He was strict and devout, enforcing the ecclesiastical rules with an iron fist, but he applied the same force to politics and grazing.

Marsden was not only the religious leader of the colony of New South Wales — he was also a magistrate. In this latter capacity he was known for severe punishments — he was particularly fond of the lash, which could be administered for simply failing to attend church.

The spiritual side of Marsden's character deplored the lax models of early Sydney town and he did his best to enforce sobriety and chastity outside marriage. His sensibilities were also inflamed by the activities of community leaders like Governor Lachlan Macquarie, who entertained the company of ex-convicts.

Marsden was born in 1764 as the son of a Yorkshire blacksmith and he was apprenticed into the trade before being called to the Anglican mission. Ironically his mentor was William Wilberforce, the social reformer known for his compassion and advocacy of the underdog. Marsden took up Wilberforce's suggestion of going to New South Wales and was quickly ordained. He arrived at Sydney in March 1794 as a deacon.

Marsden was first posted to Norfolk Island (at that time a penal colony) for a year and then returned to Sydney as assistant to Reverend Richard Johnson. He was aggrieved at the terms of his

The Mad — The Larrikins and Eccentrics

appointment and his power in the colony. His displeasure was mollified by grants of land near Parramatta, where he grew sheep and some crops. He was the first Australian grazier to ship wool to England.

No doubt growing up poor and Methodist in England shaped Marsden's views. He believed that wealth was next to godliness and his accumulation of treasure on earth was a symbol of his piety. He also believed that sinners stayed sinners, and thus opposed Governor Macquarie's policies of emancipating convicts. He was a believer in hard work as a means of pleasing God and thought this especially true of his convict slaves.

While at Norfolk Island, Marsden had met some Maoris. He then became interested in New Zealand and made seven trips across the Tasman to establish a mission on the North Island. This was an important step in the settlement of New Zealand; however, contemporaries questioned Marsden's motives as being more influenced by trade than salvation of the natives.

Marsden quickly entered the upper echelon of the colony of New South Wales. Nonetheless, he was a belligerent personality who soon fell foul of Macquarie. His other archenemy was James Macarthur, the colony's major wool entrepreneur, with whom Marsden fought at every opportunity. In turn, Macarthur and Macquarie thwarted Marsden wherever possible. Macquarie refused to allow him to return to England for business visits.

Marsden was, in fact, more popular in London where his friends didn't see his unpleasant side. King George III was sufficiently impressed with Marsden's gift of a wool suit that he sent him a flock of royal Merino sheep. Marsden's contribution to the wool industry was significant — certainly more notable than his spiritual work — and was achieved more by solid work than the more scientific approach of the Macarthurs.

Marsden's chief pastoral issue was a fight with Macarthur, who worked his convicts on the Sabbath.

However, Marsden was mostly known as a magistrate, and he dispensed justice harshly. He had a dim view of the morals of the convicts and thought flogging was not good enough for them, but he didn't waste too much time on their souls either, as he thought they were beyond redemption. He was not above torture, and in 1880 had a man almost flogged to death in order to secure information about a crime.

Marsden particularly hated Catholics and the Irish, and the division between the Anglo Saxon Protestants and the Irish Catholics was to be a major dynamic in Australia until after the World War II.

As a working-class boy made good, Marsden was snobbish and refused to sit on a magistrate's bench with emancipists. He deplored Aborigines and took their lack of interest in financial gain as evidence that they would not make good Christians.

By the time Marsden died in 1838, he had made a substantial contribution to the colony, and his high-minded intolerance and snobbery, as well as his indifference to religion and ruthless pursuit of wealth, set the tone for Australia's own religious growth.

Percival Searle, author of the *Australian Dictionary of Biography*, noted of Marsden, 'It was a cruel and intolerant age, and he was not in advance of his time.'

Daniel Patrick Mannix

If Samuel Marsden set the tone for the Protestants in Australia, almost a century later the Catholics found a champion in Melbourne.

Daniel Patrick Mannix, who was born in 1864 in County Cork, was a passionate Irish nationalist, a social democrat and a political meddler until the day he died at the age of ninety-nine.

Mannix was educated by the Christian Brothers and ordained in 1890. An ultra-orthodox priest, in 1912 he was consecrated as bishop and sent to Melbourne, where in 1917 he became archbishop.

While Mannix believed in the doctrine from Rome, Dublin came a close second. His professional enemy was Satan, but he was sure the Devil was an Englishman. His hatred of the English brought him notoriety in a country that was deeply divided along sectarian lines. Australian Catholics were discriminated against, especially in the senior ranks of the public service and the professions, and it was almost impossible for one to be accepted in the upper levels of society. Mannix championed the cause of his coreligionists and aligned it with the Irish cause for independence from Great Britain.

When the Great War broke out in 1914, Mannix spoke against Australia sending troops and in 1916 and 1917 strongly opposed Prime Minister Billy Hughes's conscription referenda.

Interestingly, Mannix's opposition to the war and to England was not much appreciated by the higher echelons of the Catholic Church. It is said that when King George V suggested that Mannix be transferred to Rome, Cardinal Gasquet replied, 'God forbid'. In 1920 Mannix visited the US and the UK, but Britain's Prime Minister Lloyd George refused him permission to land in Ireland. The Royal Navy intercepted his boat and put him ashore at Penzance, where he was kept under watch by the police and warned from going to Liverpool and other cities with large Irish populations, for fear of rioting

Under Mannix's stewardship the Catholic Church in Australia expanded fourfold and its activities, particularly in schools, flourished. His support of the working class won him influence in the ALP and he had a mutually beneficial relationship with Labor leaders such as Joe Lyons, Arthur Calwell and James Scullin. Mannix saw the ALP as the party of working-class Catholics and tended to downplay its socialist ideology, which he found an anathema. This entrenchment of Catholics in the ALP was a major factor in shaping the party and keeping it a conservative force.

Mannix had a close friendship with gambler and crime figure John Wren, who also came from poor Catholic stock and was an influential figure in ALP politics. For the first three decades of the last century the archbishop and the gambler were the two most powerful figures in Melbourne.

Mannix's other great relationship, later in his life, was with BA Santamaria, who was effectively his political adviser and theorist. Santamaria headed Catholic Action and later the Catholic Social Studies Movement (known as The Movement). They infiltrated the trade unions and by 1949 controlled the Victorian branch of the ALP, and caused the Labor Party split of 1954. Mannix's political aims were to stem the rising threat of communism and to advance the Catholic Church, especially in the area of state aid for Catholic schools.

Archbishop Mannix suffered a fatal heart attack in 1963, shortly after making his annual wager on the Melbourne Cup. It was said that he expected a long purgatory.

John Dowie

Firebrand faith healer John Dowie was born in Scotland and emigrated, with his parents, to Adelaide at thirteen. He worked for a time as a grocer, then studied for the ministry and preached in Sydney, Melbourne and Adelaide, managing to alienate many in the Spiritualist and Congregationalist communities in all three cities.

Dowie married his cousin and set sail across the Pacific to try his luck in the land of the free and the home of modern fundamentalism. Though it must be said that he was ahead of his time — even turn-of-the-century Pentecostalism had yet to gain a foothold when he arrived in the United States.

After a two-year stopover in San Francisco Dowie landed in Chicago, where his aggressive brand of Christianity finally found fertile ground. Word spread that at his sermons the lame threw away their crutches and walked, which drew the ire of the medical profession but attracted capacity crowds.

In 1896 Dowie created the Christian Catholic Apostolic Church in Zion and in 1901 he founded Zion City about 60 kilometres outside of Chicago. In 1904 he launched a mission to convert the world and his trip to Dublin is mentioned in James Joyce's *Ulysses*. There were, however, already rumblings of dissent among his followers, and while he was on tour in Central America in 1906 a rebellion (in which even his family took part) deposed him from roles of leadership in the community. Dowie lived for another year, in failing health, on an allowance from the church which he had created. He died in March 1907.

Although somewhat discredited by his initial church, Dowie is still considered one of the founders of the Pentecostal tradition in the United States.

Charles Webster Leadbeater

Charles Webster Leadbeater is one of the few people in the twentieth century who can claim to have discovered a messiah and

The Mad — The Larrikins and Eccentrics

founded a global religious cult. A controversial figure on four continents, Leadbeater was a significant presence on the Sydney scene between the wars. But by then he was no longer welcome in polite society elsewhere in the world.

Born on 17 February 1847 in England, Charles was ordained as an Anglican priest in 1879 and had a small Hampshire parish. There, living with his mother, he pursued two lifelong interests: astronomy and the company of teenage boys.

Leadbeater became interested in theosophy, the esoteric religion founded by Madame Helena Petrovna Blavatsky, which was a mixture of occultism, oriental religions, Christian mysticism and natural health. Theosophy and similar philosophies were very popular in the late-Victorian era, attracting some of the most eminent thinkers of their time as well as a variety of eccentrics. Leadbeater was an enthusiastic disciple, joining the society in 1883 while still a parson. A year later he hosted a party for his friends and the next morning disappeared from the parish, leaving behind money and gifts for his three favourite boys and his cat, Peter. Leadbeater claimed his esoteric study was creating doctrinal conflicts in his mind with his parish work. As he became more interested in theosophy and the spirit world, his interest in Anglicanism declined. There was some suggestion in the London newspapers that an investigation of his relationships with the boys might also have hastened his departure.

Leadbeater joined Madame Blavatsky in London and left straightaway for Cairo to develop his powers of clairvoyance.

Blavatsky considered Leadbeater to be a naturally gifted clairvoyant, conversant with many dead spiritualists and also with Martians.

From Cairo, Leadbeater proceeded to Adyar in south India, where Blavatsky and Colonel Olcott had established the society's global headquarters. Colonel Olcott engaged Leadbeater to train acolytes to achieve the astral plane, and then Leadbeater moved on to Sri Lanka, where he was confirmed as a Buddhist.

In Colombo he made the acquaintance of a young man, C Jinarajadasa, whom Leadbeater claimed to recognise as the reincarnation of his dead younger brother. C Jinarajadasa became his companion, Leadbeater paying for his education and that of another young boy.

Leadbeater was an active and popular speaker, especially on the subjects of Mars, clairvoyance and other topics that led to scandal. While on a lecture tour in the US in 1904 he gave a speech to young men on the virtues of masturbation. Questions about Leadbeater's sexuality began to be aired publicly, and the fact that he often travelled with groups of male students didn't help matters. Neither did the allegations that he personally instructed young boys on the techniques of onanism. Damagingly, two boys came forward with allegations of having had relations with him and documents were presented to the society. He left the US swiftly under a cloud.

The Theosophical Society was a savagely political organisation. Leadbeater was close to Annie Besant, a major figure in the movement after the death of Madame Blavatsky; however, they fell out when scandal descended on Leadbeater.

The Mad — The Larrikins and Eccentrics

Following the scandal in America, Colonel Olcott accused his friend of being a homosexual and paedophile and accepted his resignation from the society. Besant also distanced herself from Leadbeater in order to gain the presidency of the society on Olcott's death in 1907. In 1908 Besant welcomed Leadbeater back into the society — she needed as many supporters as she could find to shore up her position — and he moved to Adyar, never to return to England. The relationship between them was one of political convenience and was never again warm.

In Adyar in April 1909, Leadbeater noticed the aura of a young Indian boy. After clairvoyant inspection, Leadbeater declared to Besant that Jiddu Krishnamurti was a World Teacher of the order of Moses, Buddha, Zarathustra, Christ and Mohammed. On 11 January 1911 Leadbeater founded a cult within the theosophical movement called the Order of the Star of the East, to help fulfil Krishnamurti's destiny as the reincarnation of the great teachers through material support for the young man and spreading the word of his arrival.

Despite Leadbeater's role in discovering the messiah, Krishnamurti, his father and Annie Besant all disliked Leadbeater. They accepted his claim to clairvoyance but excluded him from contact with Krishnamurti.

With settlement in England and the US both posing potential legal problems, and scandals in India having reached a point where he was no longer welcome there, Leadbeater was in virtual exile and moved to Australia to live in 1915.

The Australian theosophists were not large in number but counted amongst their supporters and members at least two prime ministers (Deakin and Barton) and many other prominent members of the community. They were never short of funds, establishing large buildings in Sydney and Melbourne and the radio station 2GB in Sydney.

Settling in Sydney, Leadbeater continued to investigate the astral plane. The mystic James Ingall Wedgwood, bishop of the Liberal Catholic Church, also came to Sydney in 1915 and 1916. He initiated Leadbeater into Masonry and the Egyptian Rite of Memphis and Misraïm, and in the Temple of the Rose and the Cross, and made him a bishop of the Liberal Catholic Church.

In 1921 the followers of the Order of the Star of the East built a massive amphitheatre at Balmoral Beach in Sydney to prepare for a spiritual happening, the arrival of the Star of the East. Leadbeater built himself a massive mansion in Mosman, on Sydney Harbour, known as 'The Manor'. Clearly there was no shortage of funds for research into the invisible, the human colony on Mars and Leadbeater's esoteric sciences.

Sydney was, in the early 1920s, at the epicentre of the global cult of the Liberal Catholic Church. However, scandal found Wedgewood, who was accused of being an adulterer, and Leadbeater, who never shook off allegations of paedophilia. There were rumours surrounding Leadbeater's initial relations with Krishnamurti, fuelled by the Indian boy's father's allegations and attempts to wrest back his son from the control of the Order of the Star of the East.

The Sydney police investigated Leadbeater more than once and found no evidence of sexual misconduct, though it was noted that he had a boy in his bath and his bed at all times to monitor his health. No less than Aliester Crowley described him as a 'senile sex-maniac'.

In his day Leadbeater was considered to be amongst the world's greatest seers. Disciples flocked to him in Sydney from all parts of the globe.

However, his reputation and that of theosophy was damaged in 1929 when Krishnamurti announced that he was not, in fact, a prophet of any kind and that the way to truth was 'pathless'.

Leadbeater was undeterred by this setback, remaining steadfastly committed to the ineffable until his death in Perth at age eighty-six. His last words were recorded as being, 'Go on, go further, keep your enthusiasm.'

William James Chidley

Sex and religion are often linked. The Sydney-based philosopher William James Chidley, who blamed the miseries of the world on his penis, propounded one of the most interesting reconciliations between the spirit and the flesh.

The Victorian era into which Chidley was born was renowned as a time of sexual repression. A great many of the leading lights of the medical and theological establishments believed that sex was the cause of most of humanity's ills. Chief among evils was masturbation, which led to blindness, madness and the like. Many authorities were of the view that the male erection was, in fact, a perversion.

William Chidley was susceptible to these ideas as a young man. He was said to have bruised his member to blackness trying to suppress the urge to masturbate, nonetheless, he succumbed to the temptations of French postcards, prostitutes and later his common-law wife, Ada, but not without considerable guilt.

In middle age, having led a full and active life, he was diagnosed with consumption. Chidley fought the disease with abstinence from intercourse, a diet of fruit and nuts, and an insistence on wearing only cotton clothing. His disease cured, Chidley was emboldened to develop his own philosophy.

While lying naked next to Ada one day, William Chidley's detumescent member found its own way to its destiny and only then became fully aroused. Chidley had discovered 'natural coition' — what he called a mixture of 'gravitation, air pressure, and peristaltic action'.

'They inhale from each other's lungs,' he wrote, describing the perfect couple. 'Their navels cup with electric thrills, her young vagina becomes erect and waits — like a set trap — until in that fusing embrace his unerect penis touches her clitoris, when her vagina flashes open and his penis is drawn in by pressure of air and secured by its head'. Chidley further noted that in the animal kingdom mating occurred only when the female was ripe, and he

The Mad — The Larrikins and Eccentrics

suggested that human sexual behaviour should be confined to the spring.

In his 1911 book, *The Answer*, Chidley wrote that moderation was the key to health, excessive sex being a perversion that led to unhappiness and 'stress and strain' in women. Intercourse led to insanity, misery, suicide, epilepsy, crime, opium smoking, obesity, tuberculosis, blindness, pigeon toes, loss of teeth, heart disease, diabetes, and asthma'. The problem was the 'shock of coition' and the effect that it had on the brain. Orgasm was a violent act that caused the brain to shrink and the facial muscles to contract.

'As time went by,' he wrote, 'and shocks accumulated, lesions would appear in the brain itself, in the blood and lymph, and in all glands and secretions. The normal waste and repair would become perverted, and either fat or consumption ensues. That is why people get fat or thin after marriage … And that is why people get bald and wrinkled and blind and deaf and pigeon-toed and epileptic and criminal and finally mad.

'Only men and women who have accumulated the shocks of coition for twenty or thirty years — until they are one mass of perverted functions — have cancer.'

He thought that society's ills could be cured by a return to eternal, perhaps primitive, values. He proposed that we should return to nudity. However, in deference to the law, he wore a tunic similar to that worn by the ancient Greeks.

Chidley believed in natural cotton, vegetarianism — exclusively fruit and nuts — fresh air and sunlight. He deplored money making, tight clothes, alcohol, opium, homosexuality, French postcards and the class system.

The details of natural coition and other interesting ways of living were contained in *The Answer*, which Chidley sold on the streets. He had a small band of followers; unfortunately the police were not among them, and Chidley was arrested on a number of occasions. It seemed as though it wasn't his views — which were actually not far from the mainstream of the time — but the fact that he explicitly discussed sex on the streets that put him foul of the law.

Although he was generally regarded as a likeable character of Federation-era Sydney, Chidley battled alcoholism in later life, was confined to mental institutions on several occasions and died in Sydney's Callan Park mental hospital. He wrote his own epitaph: 'Mine has been an unhappy life, but it contains a moral, namely, that all my misery comes from that "erection" in boys and men. Farewell.'

William Gocher

The early part of the twentieth century had many men worried about disrobing.

Aspiring politician and sometime journalist William Gocher was an activist for daylight bathing. Until 1902 'bathing in waters exposed to views from any wharf, street, public place or dwelling' was only permitted between the hours of 6 a.m. and 7 p.m. The regulations were to protect public decency rather than any views about safety.

In January 1902 Gocher challenged the local ordinances and bathed at noon on a Sunday. On his fourth flouting of the law he was arrested, but the charges did not proceed. It was clear to the police representative, Mr Forsby, and the magistracy that public opinion had changed and that, provided bathers were covered from neck to knee, they should be allowed on the beach. On 2 November 1903 Manly Council rescinded its restrictions on daylight surf bathing.

The *Daily Telegraph* elevated Gocher to national hero. Writing in the *Sydney Mail*, Arthur Rosenthall said that Gocher's civil disobedience had led to the public's right to surf 'without molestation ... the waters of the Pacific that wash the shores of Manly Beach'.

Leila Waddell

Australia's only High Priestess, Leila Ida Nerissa Bathurst Waddell was born in 1880, the daughter of Mr and Mrs David Waddell of Bathurst and Randwick.

She was part-Maori, a voluptuous beauty with striking features including deep brown eyes and long, dark hair that covered her breasts. She began her professional career as a violin teacher at Presbyterian Ladies College, Croydon, and Ascham and Kambala schools. She was a passable violinist who made her way on the vaudeville stage.

In 1908 Waddell was a member of the gypsy band in *A Waltz Dream* at Daly's London Theatre. While in London, Waddell met Aliester Crowley, the theosophist mystic and master of the black arts. Crowley was a self-declared representative of Satan who referred to himself as 'The Beast' and 'the wickedest man in the world'. He was notorious as a promiscuous bisexual. Leila, however, appeared to have stolen his heart. He referred to her variously as 'Divine Whore', 'Mother of Heaven', 'Sister Cybele', 'Scarlet Woman' and, most affectionately of all, 'Whore of Babylon'. They studied the occult and took mescaline together. Crowley's famous *Book of Lies* was largely dedicated to Waddell, with poems like 'Duck Billed Platypus' and 'Waratah Blossoms'.

Crowley wrote in his journals, 'I was also very busy helping Laylah [sic] in her career. The problem was not easy. I soon discovered that it was not in her to undergo the dreary remorseless drudgery demanded by ambition to the classical concert platform. Striking too as her success had been in the Rites of Eleusis, it soon became clear that its source was the impulse of my personality. I could invoke the gods into her; I could not teach her to invoke them herself.

'The truth of the matter was that her art was a secondary consideration with her. Secretly, she herself was probably unconscious of it. She was obsessed by the fear of poverty, the Oedipus-complex wish for a "secure future", snobbish ambition to improve her social standing. As soon as she passed the age of thirty and came into contact with the atmosphere of America, the spiritual and even the romantic sides of her character wasted away. She rushed desperately from one prospect of prosperity to another, only to find herself despised and duped by the men she was trying to deceive. At last she dropped to the depth of despair and in her drowning struggles lost her last link with life and love. She became a traitor and a thief; and bolted with her spoils to hide herself, like Fafnir, from the very eye of heaven.

'I failed to divine the essential hopelessness of helping her. I idealised her; I robed her in the royal vestures of romance. The power and passion of her playing inspired me. Her beauty, physical and moral, bewitched me. I failed to realise to what extent these qualities depend upon circumstances; but it was clear by the beginning of 1912 that she could never get much higher than leading the Ladies Band in *The Waltz Dream* as she had been doing. The best hope was to find something equally within her powers, which would yet give her the opportunity to make an individual impression. I therefore suggested that she should combine fiddling with dancing. My idea was, of course, to find a new art form. But of this she was not capable. She failed to understand my idea.

'I acquiesced. I turned my thoughts to making a popular success for her. We collected six assistant fiddlers, strung together a jumble of jingles and set them to a riot of motion; dressed the septette in coloured rags, called them "The Ragged Ragtime Girls" and took London by storm. It was a sickening business.'

Crowley promoted Waddell's vaudeville group on tours of Europe, the US and Russia.

When, in 1910, Crowley was named High Priest of the Ordo Templi Orientis, Leila became his high priestess. There is a striking portrait of Leila naked to the waist with her long hair covering her breasts and a magic symbol painted on her sternum.

In 1915 Crowley stood at the base of the Statue of Liberty and declared an Irish Republic in a long and impassioned speech accompanied by Leila on the violin. Waddell herself toured the US and had some success as a writer, but the relationship with Crowley disintegrated as a consequence of his infidelities. In 1923 she returned to Sydney to nurse her ailing father. Back in Sydney she performed with JC Williamson Ltd Orchestras at Her Majesty's Theatre and the Criterion, and with the Conservatorium and Philharmonic Societies Orchestras. In between times she resumed teaching, this time at the Convent School of the Sacred Heart in Sydney's Elizabeth Bay. One can only wonder, after her adventurous life, what she thought of these young girls from good families and, furthermore, what their parents would have thought had they known their daughters were being taught by a high priestess with full knowledge of the dark arts.

Leila Waddell died of cancer at the age of fifty-two, unmarried. *The Sydney Morning Herald* noted: 'Besides possessing an excellent technique, Miss Waddell's style as a violinist was particularly marked by charm and refinement.'

Rosaleen Norton

Australia's other notable woman of the black arts was also a resident of Sydney's inner-eastern suburbs. According to legend, in 1917, when Rosaleen Norton was born in Dunedin, New Zealand, there was a strip of extra skin stretching from her armpit to her waist. It appears that Norton was always interested in the provocative and the slightly occult themes, especially after she took up drawing. While her pictures have an undeniable passion and draughtsmanship, it has to be said that she was not particularly good at drawing and rarely did her imagery move above the clichéd or the banal — much like Norman Lindsay.

Rosaleen — or Roie, as she was known — was a natural bohemian. She was bisexual and, according to her biographer Neville Drury, she was sexually adventurous and liked both homosexual men and women, and sadomasochism. She married young but it did not last.

Norton's most enduring relationship was with poet Gavin Greenlees. The other love of her life was the god Pan, whom she worshipped relentlessly.

In the years between the wars Norton was a bohemian artist and contributor to magazines like *Smith's Weekly*. She wrote Gothic fiction, modelled for Norman Lindsay and did her own work that generally wound up on the walls of pubs and cafes around Kings Cross.

Greenlees helped Norton to stage her first major exhibition, held in 1949 at the Rowden-White Gallery at Melbourne

University. The police deemed the show to be obscene and charges were laid over four pictures under the *Public Offences Act*. The police lost the case, and Norton's reputation grew.

In 1952 printer Walter Glover published *The Art of Rosaleen Norton* with poetry by Gavin Greenlees. Within weeks the postmaster-general had seized the stock and laid charges. A court found that some of the pictures were obscene and would have to be changed. Glover's supporters included Frank Packer, but in any event Glover went bankrupt over the matter.

Norton was an easy target for the tabloids as there were so few eccentric or colourful characters about whom to write. As a sometime hack herself, Norton took all the attention in her stride.

In September 1955 a girl was picked up for vagrancy in the Cross and claimed that she had been at a black mass held by Norton and was suffering the effects. She later retracted her claims, but the knives were out.

Norton was undoubtedly a serious devotee of the occult, and conducted rituals with a group of friends. The most famous of these was Sir Eugene Goossens, conductor of the Sydney Symphony Orchestra and the man who started the push for the Sydney Opera House.

Goossens returned from a trip to Europe in March 1956 and was searched by customs. Amongst his other luggage, customs officers discovered occult paraphernalia including masks used for Pan worship and 1166 pornographic images.

On 11 March the *Sunday Telegraph* reported:

The Mad — The Larrikins and Eccentrics

BIG NAMES IN DEVIL RITE PROBE.
Police investigations have disclosed that 'black masses' and other devil worship ceremonies have taken place in luxurious homes on the North Shore. A banker, a lawyer, and one or two radio artists are said to be among those involved. Police disclosures followed an intensive Sydney wide check on practising of Satanic rites. The extent of devil worship in Sydney amazed police. They are expected to make shock disclosures soon.

It's likely that the collection of erotica was very tame by today's standards. However, Goossens was fired by the Sydney Symphony Orchestra and divorced by his wife, and he returned to Europe a broken man.

Photographs surfaced of Norton and Greenlees performing sex rituals; they said that the photographs were taken in fun for a party. The thieves tried to sell the pictures to *The Sun*. The proprietor of the Kashmir cafe in Macleay Street, Potts Point, was busted for displaying Norton's work that was deemed 'lewd, lustful and erotic'.

In October 1955 their flat was raided and photographs discovered. Most revealing of all was correspondence with Goossens that described the sex rituals that had been happening amongst Norton's fellow devotees and the sexual relationship between the witch and the musician.

The trial did not bother Norton unduly, although she appeared to be disorientated and occasionally needed to take a break — this was due to the effects of the methedrine and dexedrine she had been taking.

Greenlees did not fare so well. The pressure exacerbated his mental health problems and he lost control of his mind. He was committed to a mental hospital in 1955 and in 1957 he was diagnosed as schizophrenic. He spent most of the rest of his life in hospital.

Through the 1960s Norton played up to her image as the Witch of Kings Cross. She dressed the part and kept her distinctive eyebrows arched and, indeed, eventually sold potions and charms.

As time went on, Norton gradually withdrew from the public eye. She lived most of her life near poverty and amongst a small circle of friends. She contracted colon cancer and, after a protracted battle of some nineteen months, died on 5 December 1979.

William Kamm

William Kamm is the most recent and perhaps the most notorious religious leader in Australia. It's often said that God works in mysterious ways, but that's nothing compared to the Virgin Mary: Our Lady chose a bank clerk standing in a field on the NSW South Coast to be her principal messenger on earth.

Born in 1950 in Germany, Kamm came to Australia at age four. He was eighteen when the Eternal Father first appeared to him in a vision and said that Kamm would lead the battle against the Antichrist. Since then the Virgin Mary has been appearing on the thirteenth of each month with updates in the cosmic conflict.

Our Lady gives Kamm — also known as 'Little Pebble' — prophecies, one of which being that he will be the next pope, the current pontiff being nothing more than a nightwatchman. Kamm eventually formed the Order of Saint Charbel, a 200-strong community outside Nowra where members await the end days.

There are a few stumbling blocks facing Kamm and his calling: not only has he been married and divorced but he is also a practitioner of 'mystical marriages' with teenagers; his beliefs seem somewhat at odds with canon law. His excommunication from the Church of Rome by Peter Ingham, the Bishop of Wollongong, could also pose a problem. But if the Virgin Mary calls by the house on the thirteenth of every month to chat directly, then who needs cardinals or bishops?

While awaiting the Second Coming, Our Lady prophesises to Kamm. During the Balkan wars she prophesised fighting in the former Yugoslavia; she has predicted earthquakes in Japan and fires in New South Wales.

In the spirit of this age, the Little Pebble is all about accountability: he has kept previous prophecies on his website so you can check the strike rate. For instance, in the FAQ section he deals with the inevitability of cosmic apocalypse: The comet Kohoutek was meant to cause debris from Mars to fall on France, the US and the Pacific Ocean. In the confusion 'a possibility is that the Olympics in Sydney may be stopped, or disrupted, due to the world events.' Pope John Paul was to kick off a new Reformation. 'Russia will invade Poland and Italy. An atomic bomb will be set off, which is hidden under the subway in New York City — planted there by Russia some thirty years ago. The Pope will flee the Vatican, which will be on fire. Global warfare and nuclear conflict follow plus earthquakes and volcanoes and the other battles foretold in the Book of Revelations.'

While not strictly a 'doomsday cult', the Order of Saint Charbel is predicated on Mr Kamm leading his followers through the end days. His work is aided by the support of similar cults around the world with as many as 75 000 followers globally. In Australia he has established at least three communities, the largest being the HQ in Camberwell, Victoria. Federal and state governments have kicked in too: the order has received grants of over $332,000 for its school and a $75,000 capital works grant.

Kamm's first wife, Anne, bore him four children. In Germany in 1990 he met his mystical wife, Bettina Lammerman; at the personal insistence of the Virgin and the Christ, they began a sexual relationship. God personally waived the Sixth Commandment. Kamm has also had a mystical marriage to Polish teenager Bozena Golebiowska.

While God may have waived His rules, the NSW Courts are sticking to theirs. According to the *Illawarra Mercury*, Nowra Local Court heard testimony that a woman had had sexual relations with Kamm when she was only fourteen years old and at the urging of her mother. The courts heard that Kamm chose a dozen 'Queens', some of them underage, from his community. A further twenty-seven 'princesses' were earmarked for possible sexual heaven. Kamm denied the allegations.

As to the stories of his mystic sex life, he has said, 'I've been worse than framed. Everything has been swept under the carpet. This is just another attempt to silence me, and it won't work.'

In July 2005 Kamm was found guilty of the sexual assault of a fifteen-year old parishioner. She entered into a mystical marriage with Kamm at her parents' suggestion, although she said that she did not sign on for actual sex. Kamm denied these allegations too, although his diaries included paragraphs such as: 'I have been thinking about it. You have such a sexy body. I believe we should wait til at least the end of next year to conceive a child … that does not mean that we can't make love.'

Kamm teaches that we are in the end days and that he will be the last pope, with some eighty-four wives by his side. Kamm will be Pope Peter II and 'as a little Moses he will lead the Church through the great apostasy (2 *Thessalonians* 2:3-13) and into the Glorious Reign of Christ at His Second Coming at the end of time'.

Maybe. Kamm is currently serving twelve years on carnal knowledge and rape charges in Goulburn Jail.

THE BAD — POLITICANS, FRAUDS, HOAXERS, IMPOSTERS AND THOSE WITH A FEW KANGAROOS LOOSE IN THE TOP PADDOCK

General Count McHugo

Crime comes in many shapes. On New Year's Day 1812, a boat, the *Active*, arrived in Launceston, in the north of Tasmania. Its owner announced himself as General Count McHugo, recently of India, and called on the Deputy Governor of Tasmania, Major George Alexander Gordon. Gordon was delighted to have a nobleman come calling to such a far flung part of the Empire and laid his services at the visitor's disposal.

Everyone except Gordon appeared to have twigged early on that McHugo was insane. He told Gordon that he was on a mission from London to inspect the conditions of the servicemen. Upon inspecting the troops he announced the end of many of the drills and increased the soldiers' rations. McHugo's insanity thus worked in the favour of the average Tasmanian and they saw no reason to spoil the fun.

McHugo was very free with his ship's stores and encouraged the locals to lead a more playful life. It was party time in Tasmania.

McHugo eventually arrested Gordon and had him confined to quarters. The major accepted the charges in the spirit that had sent the Light Brigade charging and even seemed unperturbed when McHugo sentenced him to death. With the Deputy Governor in prison, McHugo had charge of the town.

Fortunately Lieutenant William Lyttleton returned from his patrol in the interior of the island and quickly sized up the situation. He restored order immediately, freed Gordon and arrested McHugo, whom he despatched to Sydney, where the chief surgeon, William Redfern, pronounced 'a State of Outrageous Insanity'. McHugo was sent back to India whence he came, and finally back to London.

It was eventually discovered that the man was, in fact, Jonathon Burke Hugo, son of a tobacco merchant and claimant to the throne.

As one Colonial observer said of another conman in terms that could equally apply to Hugo/McHugo: 'Never again will he find a community like Australia — so capable of driving a hard bargain when dealing with commoners, but so easily led by the nose when they believe themselves to be honoured with the patronage of noblemen.'

John Dow

Transportation to the colonies had its merits — chief among them was getting criminals of all types as far from England as possible. The downside was that the Australian colonies had a high percentage of criminals amongst the population. The free settlers tended to be battlers — few travelled to the other side of the globe

The Bad — Politicians, Frauds, Hoaxers and Imposters

if they had better options at home. Thus distance worked in favour of imposters and frauds, and those who claimed proximity to the British aristocracy did best of all. The settlers were overjoyed and starstruck to be in the presence of real 'gentlemen'.

John Dow was transported to Tasmania for seven years. After serving his sentence he transformed himself into Edward, Viscount Lascelles, eldest son of the Earl of Harewood and distantly in line to the throne of England.

Dow had done his homework: the Earl of Harewood was a prominent and wealthy British politician. His son Edward had married 'a common prostitute' and disappeared in Germany after being disinherited by his father.

The Sydney Lascalles was careful to look the part, bedecked in jewellery and fine clothes and the Harewood insignia. He went about his business making notes about life in the colony and being feted around town by all manner of citizens keen to have their voice heard back home.

In 1833 he made the local headlines after he embarked on an affair with one Lilius Dickson and they spent three days together at a hotel in Parramatta. Eventually her family came and took her home. Lascelles responded with a writ of *habaeus corpus*, demanding her return. He claimed that 'he and Miss Dickson entered into a marriage contract, which had been consummation affected — that she had lived with him as man and wife, and that she had repeatedly acknowledged him in the presence of witnesses to be her lawful husband.'

Unable to corroborate the marriage, however, Justice Dowling in the Supreme Court denied the application. To his embarrassment it happened that Miss Dickson was also seeing his nephew Willoughby.

According to Dowling, 'She was one of the natural children of a miller named John Dickson, who had resided many years in New South Wales, leaving his wife in Scotland. He had cohabited many years with another woman and lived with her in Sydney, and had several children by her — Lilius Dickson being one. Her mother was a convict as I was told, but this is doubtful. Dickson was a notorious atheist, and otherwise a person of questionable reputation. I was privately informed of the fact by Dr Bland, that Lascelles had clandestinely paid his addresses to Lilius; that this fact being discovered by the father, the latter flew into a rage, and struck his daughter with a chair. Thereupon she left her father's house, and placed herself for one night under the protection of Lascelles, who next day delivered her up to her father at the intercession of the Doctor. It was understood and believed that nothing improper in fact took place between the lady and Lascelles during this interval.'

The following year, in January 1934, the viscount turned up at the property of Francis Prendergast near Windsor on Sydney's northwest. He explained that he was on a mission from the British government to inspect the colonies and to report on the system of transportation. To Mr Prendergast and others he explained that much of his travelling was done incognito for national security reasons.

Prendegast made the viscount welcome for a fortnight. 'Lascelles' made use of the Prendergasts' house, their horses and their larder. On one of his trips to Blacktown he purchased horses, and paid for these — and the Prendergasts' hospitality — with cheques. Unfortunately, the cheques bounced.

Lascelles could not last much longer. News reached the real Earl of Harewood and the forgeries in Sydney came home to roost. In May 1835 Dow aka Lascelles was found guilty of forgery and sent back to Tasmania for another seven years.

Lewis Lasseter

Lewis Hubert Lasseter was born in Victoria in 1880 and from an early age invented himself. He claimed to have left home at the age of nine; certainly, by the age of seventeen he was committing petty crime and was sentenced to eighteen months in reform school. His own accounts of this age, however, put him discovering a massive 'reef' or seam of gold that measured a mile and was situated in central Australia, near the border between Central and Western Australia. He claimed to have come upon it in 1897 and again in 1900.

In 1911 Lasseter first raised funds to mount an expedition to find the lost gold reef but the party was forced to turn back. Lasseter claimed that there was no map that showed the location of the reef but he knew that he could find his way back there on a mixture of memory and instinct.

In his twenties Lasseter travelled the world and married for the first time. He was a man ready to apply himself to any task, full of schemes, plans and designs. He and his young family moved to the NSW North Coast, where he grew fruit and other produce. Even here he was full of ideas for improvement of bridges and the like. At one point he claimed to have designed — in 1913, almost twenty years before it was built — the Sydney Harbour Bridge.

At the outbreak of the World War I Lasseter tried to enlist in the Army but was judged medically unfit. He later claimed to have served at Gallipoli but this was clearly unlikely — Lasseter always had an ambiguous regard for the truth. Mostly he found work as a casual journalist.

In 1924 Lasseter married for a second time. He didn't settle down, instead he travelled extensively in search of his calling and was forever proposing ideas to solve local issues. Some of these ideas included setting up an advanced defence, based in Far North Queensland, to protect against in invasion by Japan (more than a decade before the Pacific War); a hydroelectric scheme for Gippsland; underground cabling of electricity and telecommunications; pre-stressed concrete, and the use of smokescreens in battle.

In July 1930 the Great Depression had started to bite; the idea of a large gold deposit sparked the public imagination. Lasseter was certain he could find it again and the Central Australian Gold Exploration Co Ltd (CAGE) was formed to finance the adventure. Subscribers put up £5000 each. There was sufficient capital to fund an aircraft and pilot; a large six-wheeled lorry; two experienced

The Bad — Politicians, Frauds, Hoaxers and Imposters

bushmen, Fred Blakeley and Fred Colson; a prospector, an engineer, an explorer and Lasseter.

The party departed from Alice Springs. The trip was extremely hazardous, and after the loss of one plane and almost losing the truck, Lasseter announced that they were 150 miles off course. The party lost heart at a station called Ilbilba, but Lasseter, a few camels and one of the party, Paul Johns, pressed on into the Gibson Desert.

As the days went on, Johns thought that the explorer was becoming increasingly erratic. One evening Lasseter returned to the camp and announced that he had found the reef but refused to tell Johns where it was. Things got heated. Lasseter pulled a pistol on his companion. There was a fight and at the end of it Johns left two camels behind and went back to civilisation.

Lasseter was never heard from again.

Tracker Bub Buck led a group of experienced trackers in search of Lasseter. They found his corpse in a cave with his false teeth and his pistol, and his diary buried nearby. According to the notebook he had come across a group of nomadic Aborigines, the Myalls, who had taken him with them after his camels had run off. However, the climate and hunger had defeated him. His last known message was carved into a tree at the Western end of the Rawlinson Range — it was the date '2. 12. 30'.

Buck suggested that the large seam of mica quartz in that area had fooled Lasseter into believing it was gold. Whatever the reality, the myth of Lasseter's gold reef, a precious seam in the dead heart of Australia, has become a part of the national mythology. Dozens of people have followed his quest.

Roger Tichborne

Australia's greatest fraudster was the talk of Victorian London for some twenty years and was immortalised by Charles Dickens and Mark Twain. In October 1865 a lawyer in Wagga Wagga, New South Wales, solved one of the controversial missing persons cases of the Victorian era. He claimed that his client Thomas Castro, a local butcher, was in fact Roger Charles Tichborne, a member of the British aristocracy and the heir to substantial estates in the United Kingdom.

Tichborne had been an adventurer who disappeared during the sinking of the *Bella* off South America in 1854. The ship was lost with all hands. Nonetheless his mother, Lady Henrietta Felicite Tichborne, refused to believe that her son was dead. She devoted her efforts and her money to finding the lost Roger.

Roger Tichborne was a member of a very established family. He was educated in France and had served in the British military as an officer. When last heard from he had been on his way to India. However, after the *Bella* was sunk no one had heard from him.

Then lawyer William Gibbes responded to an advertisement in the newspaper placed on behalf of the now-widowed Lady Henrietta. According to Gibbes, Tichborne called himself

The Bad — Politicians, Frauds, Hoaxers and Imposters

Thomas Castro and had lately operated a business as a butcher in Wagga. He had been living incognito but was now ready to come forward.

There was much excitement at this revelation, especially since Tichborne was in line to inherit the ninth-largest fortune in Britain.

All sorts of people came forwards to be Tichborne's friends and supporters. Tichborne and his family took to the aristocratic life of parties in his honour and good food and wine. Given that Tichborne was broke, funds were raised for him to travel to Sydney and thence to London. Many people were prepared to extend him credit, and the dowager Tichborne sent £200 for his passage home.

While in Sydney, Tichborne met Andrew Bogle, a former member of the Tichborne household. Bogle had been born a slave in Jamaica and was freed by the Tichborne family and worked as their servant. Bogle and Michael Guilfoyle, a Tichborne gardener, both recognised Castro as Roger Tichborne.

Bogle offered his services as valet to Roger Tichborne. He was able to provide information to the missing heir about the family history; his past and the general lay of the land. It was an invaluable association — made even more so because Bogle's son had lent Tichborne money. And there was little chance of getting money back from Tichborne unless he succeeded in inheriting.

In early 1856 the new Roger Tichborne met Lady Tichborne in Paris and was immediately recognised as her long-lost son. Lady Henrietta had always been at war with her family and she hated

England —she may have well been a little mad. She was, however, convinced. Castro was, to say the least, surprised. He went along for the ride and it never seemed to stop.

The fact of the matter was that Castro, who was called the Tichborne Claimant, had no physical resemblance to Roger. He could barely speak English, whereas Roger Tichborne had been fluent in both English and French and a very capable writer. Tichborne had none of the signs of breeding that an English aristocrat would have.

It was soon suggested that he wasn't even Thomas Castro, that his name was Arthur Orton and he had been born at Wapping, London, on 20 March 1834. He had taken up his father's trade of butchery after a couple of years of school. Like Tichborne, he had set off for a new life in the South Seas, arriving in Tasmania in 1853. He had travelled around Australia before settling in Wagga Wagga with a wife who was even less sophisticated than he was.

This story didn't sway Lady Henrietta, though, and Tichborne/Castro/Orton then set about claiming his estates.

Now ensconced in London, there was no shortage of people who wanted to get to know this controversial figure. When the Tichborne family monies were turned off, a number of financiers where prepared to stake the claimant in his suit, no doubt in expectation of a percentage of the result.

People from all walks of life came forward to identify the claimant as Sir Roger; these tended to be ex-soldiers and servants.

The Bad — Politicians, Frauds, Hoaxers and Imposters

The family steadfastly remained unconvinced. The family physician, Dr Lipscombe, did however announce that the claimant was Sir Roger — one of his verifying points was that they both possessed a retractable penis.

The claimant took the matter to the courts in a protracted and convoluted case that had London obsessed. The claimant was his own worst enemy, often getting drunk, behaving in a singularly unaristocartatic manner and making outrageous claims. He sponged off everyone he met. But a large of number of people were depending on him winning the suit, so he sold Tichborne Bonds that guaranteed the investment. The claimant became something of a working-class hero and appeared frequently at rallies. After the dowager's death in 1888, as funds became even harder to come by, the claimant stepped up his touring. It was estimated that if the claimant had been successful his debts were so great that the ninth-largest estate in England would have to be sold to pay them.

'I could not get away from those who were infatuated with me and firmly believed I was the Real Sir Roger,' he wrote. 'Of course I knew perfectly well I was not, but they made so much of me, and persisted in addressing me as Sir Roger, that I forgot who I was and by degree I began to believe I really was the rightful owner of the estates. If it had not been that I was feted and made so much of by the colonialists in Sydney I should have taken the boat and gone the rest of my days to Panama with my brother.'

In 1872 the courts found against the claimant, going so far as to have him charged with perjury on account of his being Arthur Orton.

That trial ended in February 1874 with a sentence of fourteen years. The Tichborne litigation was the longest-running case in British legal history. It was a major issue of the day and was written about by Mark Twain, amongst many others.

The Tichborne Claimant was one of the most famous people in the mid-to-late nineteenth century; his story had all the elements of identity and class. After being released from prison, where he found Jesus Christ, the claimant died on April Fool's Day 1898, at the age of sixty-four.

The Fine Cotton Affair

When not punting himself, Harry Solomons was the chief race caller for Melbourne station 3XY. Unfortunately the remuneration for calling the races didn't cover the cost of wagering on them. In order to get square, Harry Solomons joined one of the most audacious scams in turf history.

The Berkeley Walter handicap was held at Ascot on Saturday, 16 December 1939. The race was scheduled for 5.05 p.m. and just it began associates of Solomons cut the cables for the other race callers on stations 3LO and 3DB. That left the majority of the broadcasting to Solomons on 3XY.

The Bad — Politicians, Frauds, Hoaxers and Imposters

Solomons ad libbed a story about the start of the race being held up by a horse named Buoyancy — Solomons was buying for time to watch the race. Once finished, the name of the winning horse — Buoyancy — was sent out as a cue for a national betting plunge with the SPs at 6-1.

Once the money was on — some three minutes after the race had actually finished — Solomons called the race again, this time from memory with a bit of imagination thrown in.

The ruse was not discovered until at least the next day. The plan had been a little too audacious and it was quickly unravelled. In his defence, after protesting his innocence, Solomons said, 'If it is true, it could not be criminal because it would only be defrauding starting-price bookmakers, and they are not legal anyhow.'

On the Monday following the race Solomons was charged with cutting the radio wires. Solomons was not a criminal mastermind by any stretch of the imagination — he told at least three other people at 3XY about the scam. But, free on bail, he skipped the country on a false passport. He was apprehended in Fiji and returned to Australia. He served six months in Pentridge Prison.

The old horse-substitution scheme was so dumb that it's extraordinary how many people were involved in the Fine Cotton scheme. This particular horse was due to run in the Second Commerce Novice at Eagle Farm in Brisbane on 18 August 1984. Its chances were judged to be 33-1. Bold Personality, however, was a winner. And, with a bit of white paint, Bold Personality became Fine Cotton.

The sudden rush of brilliance from the nag 'Fine Cotton' was accompanied by a $1.5 million betting plunge that narrowed the starting price to 7-2. Somebody knew something. Fine Cotton's trainer, Hayden Haitana, didn't stick around to illuminate anything. He told the South Australian police a fortnight later, 'I thought, well, I'm in big trouble here … 'cause at, by that time pandemonium broke out, people are jumping the fence and yelling "Ring in", and all that so, I thought I'm gone, you know, I didn't even get to pat the horse when it come in.'

Haitana claimed that organised crime figures had forced him into the scam and the recent murder of another trainer, George Brown, had focused his attention.

'They thought that if they got hair colouring and, um, got enough to fill up a couple of buckets, you could cover the horse with it, to, to make it look like., Fine Cotton,' he said. 'But as it turned out [paint] doesn't take to horse's hair, there must be a chemical disbalance there somewhere. So, ah, they just went ahead and tried to paint its white feet brown, but the horse come out red like a Hereford bull so, I couldn't believe it though.'

'I can see the look on the face of one of the jockeys who was sitting in the jockeys' room. Smiling broadly,' recalled former Cabinet minister Jim Killen. 'And I said, "What on earth's going on?" "Oh," he said, "Jimmy, there's a ring-in." I said, "Oh cut it out, please, a ring-in here … at Eagle Farm?"'

John Schreck, known as 'the Sheriff' investigated the matter for the Australian Jockey Club. He found that one punter; Ian Murray, had laid over $50 000 on Fine Cotton. Murray was off trekking in the wilds of Tasmania when the investigation turned to him. Undaunted, Schreck set off in pursuit and finally found the punter's camp.

'It was freezing cold, a big raging fire going, and he and I went a bit away from the rest of the group and chatted with a couple of big thick scotches, trying to keep warm in this Tasmanian, mountain weather,' Schreck recalled. 'And he decided that it was in his interests, his family's interests, and racing's interests generally to come back and, give evidence …'

The investigation also led to bookmakers Bill and Robbie Waterhouse, who were then among the most respected bookmakers on the Australian turf. They were 'warned off' all Australian racecourses. The phrase 'warned off' has a venerable tradition dating back to the reign of King Charles II, who 'warned off' his track those who were 'undesirable on the turf and unfit to associate with the gentlemen of the turf'.

After seventeen years Robbie Waterhouse was finally allowed back at the track and even resumed his bookmaking licence. Haitana and one John Gillespie were jailed

Arthur Coningham

Arthur Coningham was an all-rounder. As a cricketer he was known as a left-handed batsman and a fast bowler, but it was not the cricket pitch that made him famous. His only tour of Britain, in

1893, was mostly notable for his off-field bravery when he saved a boy from drowning in the Thames. His career highlight came when he represented Australia in the 1894/5 tests against England in Melbourne.

Coningham, who was born in 1863, was given to colourful behaviour. After being no-balled in his first Test, in a fit of temper he hurled the ball at the English captain. He is also said to have lit a fire in the outfield to keep warm while fielding.

He soon moved to other trades; firstly as a chemist and later a bookmaker, carrying a satchel that announced 'Coningham the Cricketer'. Shortly before leaving for Britain in 1893 Coningham married the teenage Alice, a nice Catholic girl who had already been pregnant to another man but miscarried. This last fact would come back to haunt the couple.

In 1900 Coningham, a Protestant — now living in Sydney — claimed that he thought his wife was unfaithful to him. When pressed she confessed that she had been having an affair with the Reverend Dennis O'Haran of St Mary's Cathedral. O'Haran was the principal private secretary of Cardinal Moran. Alice also revealed that her third son, Vincent Francis, was in fact O'Haran's child. She detailed the affair in the press and revealed that most of the sexual acts were conducted within the confines of the cathedral buildings. Coningham asserted that there was a strong resemblance between Vincent and O'Haran and most observers agreed with him.

Coningham wrote to Cardinal Moran demanding a divorce and

damages to his reputation of £5000. The Cardinal called it blackmail and the matter was sent to court.

Until relatively recently, Australia had been a nation viciously divided along Catholic and Protestant lines. The Coningham divorce case was more than just a marital breakdown: the trial was a major scandal out of all proportion to the public stature of any of its participants. The Catholic community saw it as a clear attack on their church and community.

Divorce proceedings in those days were recorded word for word; the closest the population had to soap opera. Coningham — proving the adage that a man who represents himself in court has a fool for a client — led his own case. He publicly pursued all the gory details.

The case took a bizarre turn when Coningham reconciled with his wife and resumed their conjugal relations while still running divorce proceedings against her. It has never been clear whether this odd behaviour stemmed from Coningham's unquenchable love for Alice or a sense of responsibility for the children. The church seized on Coningham's behaviour and claimed that it merely proved that Coningham was only after a financial settlement from the church and was not really aggrieved at all.

Coningham replied with long theological arguments peppered with anti-Catholic rhetoric. He was not just prosecuting adultery; he was rerunning the Reformation and the church countered. At one stage Justice Owen, also a Protestant, threatened to have the cardinal jailed for contempt. The matter was eventually called a mistrial and the opponents regrouped in their corners for a second round.

Cardinal Moran took no chances with the retrial: he engaged William Crick, who was a solicitor, member of parliament and postmaster-general, as part of the defence team. Crick employed an agent, Dan Murphy, who planted spies to befriend Coningham and to investigate his wife, who had now moved out of town. Crick used his office as postmaster-general to intercept and read all of Coningham's mail.

The church had suspected that Coningham had a supporter amongst its ranks supplying him with information. Letters had gone from someone close to the cardinal to Coningham, giving him clues and facts for investigation. Crick unmasked the fifth columnist and then took his place. Now Crick or his agents wrote the information that Coningham received. Posing as the informant whom Coningham trusted, Crick's letters told Coningham that he should date the occasions of adultery on two specific days: 1 April and 30 April.

Coningham passed the information to Alice so that she could put dates to her sworn testimony of adultery. Of course, when Alice repeated the dates in court O'Haran had ironclad alibis. The credibility of the Alice Coningham, now in doubt, was soon ripped to shreds. The matter of her illegitimate pregnancy was raised and her character was destroyed.

Moran and Crick's skulduggery paid off: the jury found for the defence and O'Haran was cleared of adultery, although few people at the time, on either side of the case, doubted that O'Haran did have the affair as stated and that Vincent was his child. Without

The Bad — Politicians, Frauds, Hoaxers and Imposters

Crick's espionage he probably would have lost the case. Father O'Haran never advanced in the church. He died in 1931 without ever lifting the stigma of the Coningham affair.

Coningham was a broken man. He had been publicly humiliated as a cuckold and his loss in court doubled his shame. One newspaper writer described him as having 'the cunning of an ape and the modesty of a phallic symbol'. He emigrated to New Zealand with Alice, where he went into the book business. In 1912 she divorced him on the grounds of committing adultery in a beach shed and this time she left. Arthur did six months in prison on a fraud charge. After returning to Sydney, he finished his days in Gladesville Mental Hospital, where he died in 1930.

Coningham's infamy was eclipsed by his eldest son's fame. Arthur Coningham II was a highly decorated flying ace in World War I. He had a very distinguished career as Air Vice-Marshal Sir Arthur Coningham, Commander-in-Chief of the Royal Air Force's 2nd Tactical Air Force in Europe. During the Second World War he pioneered the use of tactical air support and was instrumental in winning El Alamein and the Normandy invasion. He was the subject of a cover story in *Time* magazine in August 1944. Tragically, the plane on which he was a passenger, the *Arvo Tudor*, was lost on 29 January 1948 near the Azores, in the area known as the Bermuda Triangle. Alice Coningham died in Sydney in 1959.

Peter Macari

The film *English Doomsday Flight* gave English thief and fraudster Peter Macari an idea. On 26 May 1971, he called the office of Qantas and told the airline that he had planted a bomb on Qantas Flight 755 bound for Hong Kong, that the bomb was activated and would explode if the plane descended to 20 000 feet. He gave his name as Mr Brown. As proof of his intentions he said he had left an identical bomb, complete with altimeter, in a locker at Sydney's Kingsford Smith airport. 'Mr Brown' said that the only way to avoid a disaster was to pay him $500 000 in used $20 notes — and they should keep the plane in the air until the money was delivered. The money was duly delivered to a man in a van parked at the Sydney Opera House. Once safely away with the cash, Mr Brown told Qantas that it was all a hoax and they should land the plane.

Now cashed up, Macari and his boyfriend, Raymond Poynting, went on a spree that soon brought them to the attention of police. The sum of $138,000 was found in a disused butcher shop but $250,000 remained unaccounted for. It turned out that Macari had form for theft and weapons charges back in Britain, and while in Australia he had been committing further frauds on banks and car dealers using the name William Day, which was coincidentally the name of a young Englishman who had recently gone missing in Australia.

Macari served nine years of a fifteen-year jail sentence and was then deported to the UK, where he now lives.

The Bad — Politicians, Frauds, Hoaxers and Imposters

John Stonehouse

Another Briton who came to Australia to find a new identity was more unlucky than evil. By most accounts a man of considerable charm and great ambition, John Stonehouse represented the seat of Walsall North in the House of Commons. He was one of the bright stars of the resurgent Labour Party in Britain during the 1960s. He aspired to move to 10 Downing Street but got only as far as postmaster-general.

Labour leader Harold Wilson didn't think much of Stonehouse's abilities and he especially didn't approve of the MP's womanising. Stonehouse took to the swinging '60s with gusto and had many affairs, the most longstanding of them with his secretary, Sheila Buckley.

When the Labour Party was tossed out at the 1970 general election, Stonehouse concentrated on his second ambition: to become very wealthy. He embarked on a number of business ventures, often using parliamentary influence and connections to further these projects, which included a bank in Bangladesh. Unfortunately, none of the schemes was profitable — quite the opposite. So Stonehouse resorted to fraudulently obtaining money and then later the cooking the books.

By early 1974 his personal affairs were in a chronic state; the authorities were beginning to investigate. It was then that he devised a plan of escape.

After reading the thriller *The Day of the Jackal* by Frederick

Forsyth, Stonehouse acquired two false passports and bled all of his companies of cash which he then stashed around the world.

In mid-1974 he took a trip to the US and staged his disappearance by leaving his clothes on Miami Beach and escaping in a second set of clothes. The plan was foiled when he lost his nerve. Then, a fortnight later, he again tried the ruse and this time he made it all the way to Australia.

It was assumed that Stonehouse had committed suicide. Sheila Buckley said that he liked to swim alone and after an extensive search the police declared him dead. The FBI, suspecting a mob hit, dug up an entire concrete car park to no avail. Stonehouse's wife, Barbara, was distraught. *The Times* ran an obituary. But MI5 were less convinced: they believed that Stonehouse had defected to the USSR.

Once established in Melbourne, Stonehouse continued to draw money out of the UK accounts he had set up under false names. By sheer coincidence, a clerk in his local Melbourne bank thought that Stonehouse might be Lord Lucan, a British aristocrat on the lam. The 7th Earl of Lucan had recently bludgeoned his nanny to death, thinking she was his wife, and he had run off. Lucan's disappearance was headline news around the world, with Australia considered a likely destination for the fugitive peer.

So the bank clerk alerted the local police, who in tern called Scotland Yard and Interpol. Stonehouse was put under surveillance.

Stonehouse then made a trip to Europe to meet Buckley and returned to Australia where, on Christmas Eve 1974, he was arrested. Stonehouse clarified that he was not Lucan but, rather, a member of parliament.

He declined to return to the UK and, as he had not committed any offence in Australia, the Australian government had no excuse to deport the MP. Barbara Stonehouse flew to her husband's side, although when Buckley also turned up this became a difficult situation. Mrs Stonehouse soon returned to the UK and filed for divorce.

Stonehouse eventually returned to Britain in January 1975 and was interred in Brixton Prison until the following August — but he remained an MP. Eventually released on bail for fraud charges, Stonehouse went back to work. He was shunned by the Labour Party which could nevertheless not evict him.

The fugitive MP used Parliament to speak of his split personality and the mental illness that had caused his erratic behaviour. In April 1976 he finally resigned from the party, putting James Callaghan's government — which had taken control of the House only days before — into a minority position. A free agent now, Stonehouse joined the English National Party, whose policies included a sixteen-lane tunnel under the Thames and the abolition of income tax.

Eventually Stonehouse faced trial and defended himself. He was found guilty and sentenced to seven years. His mistress, Sheila Buckley, was given a suspended sentence. The English National Party urged Stonehouse not to resign his seat 'in view of his vital position as the only MP representing England and her 46 million people'.

Stonehouse served three years in jail; his sentence was reduced on the basis of his ill health. On his release in 1981 he married Buckley and settled down with her, eventually fathering a child (he already had a daughter by his first wife). Stonehouse dedicated his final years to writing and public speaking.

Donald Cameron

The desire for new identity is a common theme before the courts. Donald Cameron knew he was destined to be a doctor, and was so convinced of his calling that he decided he didn't need a university degree to do it … His career of impersonation and false pretences started as far back as 1961 and continued until 1978, in spite of a total of twenty-four years spent in jail.

In the late 1960s Cameron impersonated a doctor and turned up for work at various hospitals. His confidence was sufficient to get him onto the wards, where he successfully treated a number of patients over several years.

In search of stability, and a steady job, he changed his name by deed poll to Patrick Thompson, in doing so stealing the identity of a qualified doctor. In 1974 he joined the medical team sent to Darwin to assist with the aftermath of Cyclone Tracey. While in Darwin Cameron/Thompson delivered, according to some sources, eighty-nine babies.

Over his career Cameron practised medicine in Melbourne,

The Bad — Politicians, Frauds, Hoaxers and Imposters

Sydney, Brisbane, London and Edinburgh. He was, by many accounts, a popular lecturer at universities in those cities, and he successfully operated on cancer patients at Sutherland Hospital in Sydney.

Things became complicated in 1979 when Cameron opened a practice in the Sydney suburb of Cronulla and a colleague of the real Patrick Thompson blew the ruse.

Cameron was sentenced to two years in prison for his efforts. 'The defendant appears to be obsessed with the medical field and believes he is competent to practise as a doctor,' police told the court.

Jail taught Cameron some lessons: he gave up medicine and took to the cloth as the pastor of the Church of Love and Peace. And the law proved to be a better profession. Shortly after his release he began to practise law, although again he didn't bother with examinations or qualifications.

In the 1980s Cameron established the Remedial Justice Association in Toowong in Brisbane and among his clients were high-profile members of the One Nation party.

Cameron even took imaginary silk, representing — as QC — a couple in the Federal Court. He came unstuck in 1992 when representing farmers George and Stephanie Muirhead in a high-profile case. Prison officials recognised him on the nightly news and he was returned to jail.

Cameron has repeatedly applied to be admitted as a barrister since then. Like many people, he has had his problems with the banks and ran, at one stage, thirteen actions against Westpac until he was declared a vexatious litigant.

The Weeping Woman

On Monday, 3 August 1986 the security guards at the National Gallery in Melbourne discovered that their prized possession, *Weeping Woman* by Picasso, had been stolen. The 55 cm x 46 cm oil on canvas painting had been purchased the previous year for $1.6 million.

The security team concluded that the painting had disappeared the previous Saturday and its absence had not been noted on the Sunday. The exact details of the robbery are a mystery to this day, but it appeared that the thieves hid in plain sight as visitors. They used a special device, known as a security tool, to unscrew the painting from the wall then cut the canvas from its frame, disposed of the frame and rolled up the Picasso and left with it under their clothing.

Students of art history as well as master thieves, the robbers' heist was an homage to the theft of the *Mona Lisa* from the Louvre in 1911.

Shortly after the loss was discovered, the gallery received a note from a group calling themselves 'Australian Cultural Terrorists'. The note suggested that the heist had been staged because of the low level of arts funding. They wrote that 'We've stolen the Picasso as a protest against the niggardly funding of the fine arts in this hick state and against the clumsy, unimaginative stupidity of the distribution of that funding.' The group demanded that in return for the painting Victorian Arts Minister Race Mathews increase arts funding by 10 per cent over three years and establish a $25 000 annual art prize called the 'Picasso Ransom'. They threatened to burn the painting if their demands were not met.

Two weeks passed before National Gallery Director Patrick McCaughey received a phone tip-off that sent him to the studio of a young artist. The police declined to get involved with this lead and so a nervous McCaughey and a colleague went along. The man in question claimed to have no knowledge of the theft and he couldn't be linked to the robbery.

Two days later *The Age* newspaper received an anonymous phone tip that the painting was in a locker at Spencer Street Station. 'We ran down from *The Age*, which is just across the road, of course, with enormous expectation, and then sort of came to a skidding halt in front of the locker,' journalist Margaret Symonds recalled for the ABC's *Rewind* program. The journalists called McCaughey, who rushed to the station as fast as he could. 'And nothing happened for twenty minutes. So it was a mixture of tension and almost slapstick, really. But yes — McCaughey was very emotional.' Help was summoned to break open the locker. The painting was intact — and the arts remain underfunded.

Wanda Koolmatrie

The visual arts are not the only victims of shams and fraud. There have been a number of famous literary hoaxes, but perhaps the most controversial crossed a number of political hot spots. In 1994 the publication of *My Own Sweet Time* was hailed as the birth of a significant new voice in Australian literature. The author, Wanda Koolmatrie, was said to be a middle-aged Aboriginal woman, a survivor of the stolen generation. Koolmatrie claimed to have been born in the far north of South Australia in 1949. She was removed from her Pitjantjara mother in 1950 and raised by foster parents in the western suburbs of Adelaide. She married Frank Koolmatrie, who died several years later.

Magabala, a Broome-based publisher run by Aborigines, believed the book to be a memoir and the small publishing house enthusiastically championed Koolmatrie. Their enthusiasm was well founded: not only was the book a critical success but it won the 1996 Nita May Dobbie Award for the best first novel by an Australian woman. Author Dorothy Hewitt said, 'This is the lively, gutsy story of an urban Aboriginal girl making it in the tough city counterculture of the mid-'60s. This heartwarming comic odyssey cries out for a sequel. It could be the start of a new genre'.

Koolmatrie had until this point wished to stay out of the public eye; she let her prose do the talking. Not even the publishers had ever seen their prize-winning author.

Koolmatrie actually was the nom de plume of Leon Carmen — a 47-year-old white male. He took Dorothy Hewitt's advice and wrote a sequel entitled *Door to Door*. But Magabala kept insisting on meeting their acclaimed author and, in the end, Carmen thought he had no choice but to give himself up.

The Bad — Politicians, Frauds, Hoaxers and Imposters

Carmen grew up in Adelaide and was a member of agit-rock group Red Angel Panic, an early version of The Angels. He worked as a public servant, taxi driver and fruit picker.

As a white middle-aged male with no track record in publishing it was very difficult to get a book accepted. However, when he adopted the identity of an Aboriginal woman the literary merits of his book were accepted.

Carmen was also the victim of the absurd literary belief that 'novels' are expected to be 'autobiography'. The work of the imagination is discounted in favour of supposed veracity. A less well-written memoir is more highly regarded than a well-made piece of fiction. As Lydia Miller, director of the Aboriginal and Torres Strait Islander Arts Board, said, 'As we now discover, it is a pack of lies, because it is actually a fiction and not autobiographical, which I think immediately devalues its literary merit.'

At no point in the controversy that was unleashed the moment Carmen came out of his closet did anyone congratulate the author on his imagination and his ability to render a story about which he had no first-hand knowledge.

Nonetheless, Carmen was immediately in the middle of a storm of negativity. Publishers announced that he was a pariah — which, of course, was his status as a white, middle-aged male novelist anyway.

Carmen said, 'I created a character and breathed life into her. I can't get published, but Wanda can.'

A section of the Aboriginal community was also up in arms. Carmen was accused of identity theft and of appropriating

Aboriginal stories which were the exclusive preserves of Aboriginal writers, according to some. There is no doubt that *My Own Sweet Time* is a fraudulent autobiography but the real question remains: is it any good?

Elizabeth Kenny

Until Dr Albert Sabin's oral vaccine arrived in the 1960s, poliomyelitis (also known as infantile paralysis) was a devastating virus that crippled hundreds of thousands of people around the world. The virus generally attacked the nervous system of children, leaving their limbs mangled and distorted, oftentimes crippling the sufferer for life. With no cure, the medical treatment was usually to immobilise the limbs, and sometimes the whole body, in splints to avoid any distortion and then pray for the illness to take its course, hoping for the best.

Elizabeth Kenny was born at Warialda in New South Wales in 1880. Her father was an itinerant farmer and she travelled through the New South Wales and Queensland countryside. She began nursing as what was known as a bush nurse — she had little training but in these isolated communities she was the only hope, so she learned to be self-reliant and essentially taught herself as best she could.

After the outbreak of the Great War she enlisted in the army, serving on hospital ships. As a result of this work she was known as

The Bad — Politicians, Frauds, Hoaxers and Imposters

Sister, although she never gained the formal qualifications signified by the title.

After the Armistice she resumed bush nursing in Queensland. Kenny had developed some ideas about the treatment of polio. Rather than immobilising the limbs she started a course of very vigorous muscle development and general physiotherapy accompanied by intense heat treatments. The treatments often went for hours and sometimes weeks on end. She had little or no understanding of the virus itself but found that this regimen helped to stave off the effects of polio and to preserve muscle capacity. In part the intensive nursing that was involved in the Kenny treatment would have aided patients more than simply being consigned to a polio ward with less frequent treatment.

In 1933 an epidemic of polio swept Australia and, especially, Queensland. Kenny was inundated with patients and opened clinics around the country. She was hailed by many, including herself, as a visionary.

While several doctors were happy to work with her, the medical establishment was not. In 1938 a royal commission was established to investigate Sister Kenny and her treatments. To her incredulity, the commission found that her treatment was not sound and produced no better results than the standard treatments in hospitals.

Kenny and her supporters were incensed.

In 1940 the Queensland Government persuaded her to try her luck in the US, where she struggled for two years to be accepted. An outbreak of polio in Minneapolis left many parents desperate to try anything. Kenny set up a clinic in that city and all twenty-six of her patients recovered.

Kenny became a national hero. The President, Franklin D Roosevelt — a polio victim himself — called on her. She was, according to some polls, the second most popular woman in the US.

She wrote her autobiography, *And They Shall Walk: The Life Story of Sister Elizabeth Kenny*, in collaboration with Martha Ostenso in 1943. This was adapted for the screen as *Sister Kenny* starring Rosalind Russell, a major star at the time, in the lead role for which she won a Golden Globe award and an Oscar nomination.

In 1951 Kenny returned to the small town of Nobby, Queensland, to retire. She was still at odds with the Australian medical establishment. Although she was widely lauded in the US and Europe, in Australia she was largely shunned.

She died the following year.

According to ABC historian Michelle Arrow, 'Sister Kenny never did find a cure for polio, but she did give hope to hundreds of thousands of victims and a sense that their lives would not be wasted away. She was part charlatan. She was part messiah. She was certainly a great self-publicist who declared, "I am right and the rest of the world is wrong. I consider that I have given the United States the greatest gift she has received from anywhere." But Sister Kenny never won the acclaim where she most desired it — the land of her birth.

'Sister Kenny always felt that America embraced her in a way that Australia did not. She came back to Australia towards the end of her life, and she wanted to be buried here, but she felt America took to her more than Australians, and partly that was because she sold herself in the United States as this brash, bold Aussie woman that would do things that Americans wouldn't, and one of the keys to that was these hats that she wore. She wore these distinctive slouch-style hats that she designed herself based on a digger's slouch hat, but they were made by a Hollywood milliner, which is a lovely detail about how she saw herself.'

Christopher Skase

Fraud sometimes comes from the most respectable places and is done with accountants rather than spivs. Christopher Skase was a journalist with *The Sun News-Pictorial* and the *Australian Financial Review*. In 1974 he traded his typewriter for a role as a stockbroker with a stake of just $15 000. The era of acquisitions, mergers and asset stripping was just beginning and Skase, like Alan Bond and Robert Holmes à Court, became a corporate predator. The skill in this business was the eye for deal — buying the stock cheaply and realising the assets before moving on. It wasn't a business that required long-term corporate strategy.

Skase's holding company, Qintex, favoured high-profile real estate developments (the Mirage resorts in Queensland) and the media.

In 1984 Qintex acquired TVQ-0 in Brisbane, HSV-7 in Melbourne and ATN-7 in Sydney, as well as similar stations in

Adelaide and Perth, plus 50 per cent of Crawfords, one of the leading television production companies. At its height Qintex was valued at $2.2 billion; Skase's acquisitions led to the creation of the Seven Network out of a number of individual stations.

Corporate buccaneers like Skase lived by the principle that the next deal would cover the costs of the last; that assests acquired by them increased in value by virtue of their new owners. They then borrowed more money at the new price. These funds were needed for future acquisitions and to maintain the Skase family in the style to which they quickly became accustomed. Qintex was heavily leveraged and Skase was too (even though Qintex paid him $100 million in fees in 1989).

Skase and his wife, Pixie, were the perfect tycoon couple: handsome, tanned and healthy-looking, dressed in the pastel tones of the era. Their success was on show for all to see. Skase's office housed a glass dome containing $1 million in shredded $100 bills. His home; 'Bromley', had cost $4 million. He drove two Rolls-Royces and a BMW and relaxed on *Mirage III*, his $6 million yacht. Frank Sinatra sang at his opulent resorts.

In September 1988 Skase celebrated his fortieth birthday in the company of Queensland Premier Mike Ahern, future premier Wayne Goss and a legion of celebrities.

Then in October 1988 there was a correction in the financial markets and players like Skase tumbled. When things were going well, no one questioned the fees or the financial structures that were reaping such nice dividends for the chairman, but the

The Bad — Politicians, Frauds, Hoaxers and Imposters

end came in early 1989 when a deal to buy MGM Studios fell over.

When Qintex collapsed, questions arose as to Skase's practices. It was not that he had spent a great deal of money but the dubious methods which he had used to finance his growth came under scrutiny. Chief amongst these were the huge fees and complex financial structures put in place to Skase's direct benefit over and above that of the shareholders.

Rather than face his creditors and possibly the regulatory authorities, Skase skipped town. His personal debts were estimated at around $172 million. Qintex went down with approximately $1.5 billion in debt and exacerbated the collapse of the State Bank of Victoria.

Skase wound up on the island of Majorca in Spain, steadfastly refusing to return to Australia, having expatriated his wealth, cars and art collection to a $5 million villa with its own orchards. When the Australian Government tried to force his return, he claimed poverty and ill health and fought tooth and nail in the courts against extradition.

In 1991 the Australian Securities Commission charged him with misusing funds but Skase had no intention of answering the charges. He continued to maintain the fiction that he was ill and unable to travel. Newspapers and television crews camped out near his villa and sent back pictures of the tycoon sunning himself by the pool or taking his constitutional. It was as though he was thumbing his nose at the Australian public. On those occasions when he was required in court he arrived in the extravagant drag of an oxygen tent, looking every bit like the eccentric billionaire Howard Hughes. Television host Andrew Denton initiated a public call for a bounty hunter to go and capture Skase, and pledges were made to the tune of $250 000.

Skase liked his status as a fugitive from the law — it appealed to his sense of drama. Stories emerged via trusty lieutenants that Skase was a drama-obsessed gay man with a sham wife and an overinflated sense of himself. His version of events appeared in an autobiography in which he claimed that he was persecuted, comparing himself to Terry Waite and Nelson Mandela.

After ten years on the run, Skase died on 5 August 2001. He was, it seems, finally broke, leaving little or nothing for the faithful Pixie and his family.

'I have received evidence the equity in that house was continually remortgaged with the funds being reused as living expenses for the Skases,' said Max Donnelly, the Public Trustee who pursued Skase for a decade. 'While Skase may have been considered a good property developer, he certainly lost his touch when he went to Spain. Now I've got some answers, there's nothing to recover.

'If you asked the average man,' Donnelly summed up, '"Name an Australian fugitive", up until Skase's death, probably Skase was the only one anyone could name. But not only was he a fugitive, we actually knew where he was, and not only did the Australian public know where he was, he was on the front page of newspapers or the

The Bad — Politicians, Frauds, Hoaxers and Imposters

TVs, maintaining his innocence and saying he was sick and poor. Well, he certainly wasn't poor. And, uh … I don't really know that he was all that sick ten years ago. The property La Noria in Majorca was a beautiful mansion with orchards and swimming pools. And it was clearly a lifestyle not for the impoverished. I think, personally, he loved the media attention that went on with his own bankruptcy — the fugitive status that was given to him.'

Dr William McBride

Dr William McBride perpetrated the most famous fraud in Australia's history. At the time McBride, who was born in 1928, was one of the world's most esteemed scientists.

In 1961 McBride proved that the drug thalidomide, which was prescribed as an analgesic for pregnant women, was the cause of terrible birth defects. When published in *The Lancet* McBride's discoveries resulted in the drug being banned in Europe and Australia (it was never released in the US), although the manufacturers continued to sell the drug to pregnant women in Brazil, Italy, Japan, Sweden and Canada with full knowledge that it could harm unborn children.

Thalidomide babies were born with deformed limbs and sometimes without limbs at all. The drug also caused abnormalities in the eyes, ears, heart, genitals, kidneys and nervous system. McBride's research saved the lives and limbs of hundreds of thousands. It also put greater scrutiny on pharmaceutical companies.

McBride established Foundation 41 to continue research into issues related to pregnancy and birth defects; it was one of the most prestigious medical research institutes in Australia. McBride's attention then turned to a morning-sickness drug called Debendox (Scopolamine), which was used in the morning sickness drug Benedictin.

According to research assistant Phillip Vardy, 'Six female rabbits were dosed, one litter of offspring, foetuses from one particular rabbit, was malformed. One litter in six proves absolutely nothing. I certainly thought at the time that this was worthy of doing a lot more work, but, ah, one litter in six would be laughed out of any reputable scientific journal. Unfortunately, that work came to an end. I gave the results to Bill McBride and thought no more about it.'

Vardy and Jill French considered the research inconclusive; without their knowledge, McBride had falsified data to back his own beliefs. Two years later, their names appeared alongside McBride's in the *Australian Journal of Biological Science* damning Scopolamine. McBride testified in the US against Bendectin, citing the research, and the manufacturer Merrill Dow eventually withdrew it from sale.

'One day, a bundle of reprints arrived from an Australian journal, *The Journal of Biological Sciences*, addressed to McBride, Vardy and French,' Vardy recalled to the ABC. 'I opened the

The Bad — Politicians, Frauds, Hoaxers and Imposters

package, and there was an amazing discovery. A publication, much of which I recognised as the one that had been done earlier, but the data did not accord with what I remembered. There I am, here leafing through this fraudulent paper with my name on it. Because my name was on it, it gave me the right to pursue the evolution of the fraud and it gave me the courage to go to one of the front secretaries and ask if I could have the lead-up data to the paper, and she reached back, grabbed an orange file, gave it to me.

'I went back and checked my original data and checked the rabbit books and the laboratory books, and came to the conclusion that McBride had added additional rabbits, he had changed the dosages — I was appalled. Science is based upon the pursuit of truth, so you can't imagine reality into place, you can't construct reality into place. And here was Bill "cooking the books", so to speak, to try and prove his case. It was anathema to any scientist.

'I can't remember how I felt. I was certainly scared. There was a mixture of rage and dismay and fear. At this stage, Bill McBride had just attempted to sue the American Academy of Science because they said that he was less than a perfect scientist, for some $US15 million. Here was I holding in my hand hard evidence that Bill McBride was a fraud.'

Despite the intimidating shadow of McBride's reputation, Vardy confronted his boss.

'I said something like, "Look, Bill, this arrived while you were away. There's a lot of things about this which really concern me, and I want to talk about it." I'm rattling on, laying out the whole fraud, trying to bring the cascade of logic to an inevitable conclusion where he *has* to admit that he's constructed a fraud, but never did he do that. And he just sort of said, "Look, I'm very disappointed in this", and, ah, "I'm sure you're mistaken." Just short statements, and so we became locked into a battle, where his purpose was to deny the truth and my purpose was to reveal it. And small battles lead to bigger ones which lead to bigger ones.'

Vardy and French confronted McBride and were fired. Their appeals to the medical establishment were ignored. They sent a letter to the *Australian Journal of Biological Sciences* concerning the issue; it was never published. Unable to work, Vardy abandoned his career as a researcher. Other staff at Foundation 41 who challenged McBride on the matter were retrenched.

The ABC broadcaster Norman Swan stumbled upon Vardy's story by accident and began his own investigation. His broadcasts in 1987 caused a scandal. Foundation 41 set up an independent inquiry into the allegations in July 1988, headed by former chief justice Sir Harry Gibbs.

The committee of inquiry reported in November 1988 that McBride had deliberately falsified data and that 'Dr McBride was lacking in scientific integrity'. That then led to the complaints unit the NSW Department of Health proceeding against Bill McBride in the NSW Medical Tribunal. McBride was struck off as a doctor and the great achievements of 1961 were forever overshadowed by his hubris.

'One of the things that struck me was how thorough Norman had been in his research, and how right he'd got it,' said Vardy.

The Bad — Politicians, Frauds, Hoaxers and Imposters

'Certainly, it was fear and relief, and then there was a feeling of guilt that someone who was imperfect themselves had blown the whistle on someone else, because it's really un-Australian to dob someone in. I thought that revealing the story would be enough, but it wasn't to be. And there, on the very front page of *The Sydney Morning Herald* on one side was a photograph of William McBride, OA, CBE, MD, the lion of Australian medicine, and here was this bit player and I thought, "Oh, dear. He's going to sue me for sure".'

While Australia has never fought a war of independence, there have been some notable struggles. If none of them ever reached the stage of a full rebellion, they were nonetheless courageous acts.

Pemulwuy

Pemulwuy was born in 1756 into the Bidjigal people around Castle Hill, northwest of Port Jackson and Sydney Town. The Bidjigal were a part of the Eora tribe, who occupied much of the land around Sydney from the Hawkesbury in the north to Botany Bay in the south prior to the arrival of the European settlers.

Many Aboriginal people tried to coexist with the British and some even moved into town; Pemulwuy was not one of them. He felt threatened and resentful towards the invaders and thought it right to defend his land. His freedom fighting continued for twelve years.

In 1790 Pemulwuy speared and killed Governor Arthur Phillip's gamekeeper, John McIntyre, and Phillip ordered a posse to bring back six Bidjigal hostages or their heads. The expedition, headed by Watkin Tench, failed to find any Bidjigal — thus the legend of Pemulwuy was born. He was a hero to the Aboriginal community and a worthy adversary to the military.

Pemulwuy disappeared into the bush, where he set about organising a resistance force. For many years he sustained a campaign against the settlers around Parramatta and Toongabbie. He used ambushes and raids on farms and tactically burned crops and killed livestock.

In 1797 Pemulwuy commanded a force of up to 100 men. It's believed that some convicts may have even defected to his army. That year he led a major attack on Toongabbie and then moved towards Parramatta for another pitched battle. Pemulwuy was wounded and captured and taken to hospital with six gunshot wounds in his body. Mysteriously, however, he got out of bed and escaped back to his force, resuming his attacks.

After his successful escapes Pemulwuy attained an almost mythical status, and it was believed that he was impervious to bullets. Governor Hunter observed: 'A strange idea was found to prevail among the natives respecting the savage Pemulwuy, which was very likely to prove fatal to him in the end. Both he and they entertained an opinion, that, from his having been frequently wounded, he could not be killed by our fire-arms.'

Pemulwuy's fame was such that some white convicts abandoned

The Bad — Politicians, Frauds, Hoaxers and Imposters

the settlement at Sydney Cove and joined Pemulwuy's resistance fighters. John Washington Price, who arrived in Sydney aboard the *Minerva* early in 1800, wrote: 'He has now lodged in him, in shot, sluggs and bullets, about eight or ten ounces of lead, it is supposed he has killed over 30 of our people.'

In 1801 Governor King put a ransom of 20 gallons of spirits or a free pardon on his head — dead or alive. A year later the Aboriginal leader was caught in an ambush and killed. His body was brought back to Sydney, where it was decapitated. King said of his adversary, '[A]lthough Pemulwuy was a terrible pest to the colony, he was a brave and independent character'

Pemulwuy's head was preserved in alcohol and despatched to Sir Joseph Banks in London. Banks kept the skull at the Royal College of Surgeons in London. It was subsequently returned to Australia in the 1950s but may have been lost.

Pemulwuy's son Tedbury carried on the resistance.

Jundamurra

The Kimberley Region of northwestern Australia is a harsh territory. White settlement was possible only with the support of the Aboriginal population, although many of the traditional landowners opposed colonisation.

Jundamurra was a member of the Bunuba people and grew up around Windjana Gorge. At the nearest station, Lillimooloora,

Jundamurra came in contact with the white settlers and the police. He was eventually employed to track sheep thieves. And, in the company of a Constable Richardson, he had enormous success.

One day in 1894 the pair apprehended seventeen Bunuba people. While the captives were in chains awaiting transport south they taunted Jundamurra about his betrayal of his own people on behalf of the white invaders. Jundamurra saw the logic of their arguments and shot Constable Richardson in the head.

With his seventeen friends, Jundamurra took to the hills. They captured a wagon's load of rifles and ammunition and began a ten-year guerrilla war against the Europeans.

Jundamurra had extraordinary skill as a bushman. His attacks on the whites and the legions of army men who came north were capricious, brave and effective. He earned a mythical status amongst his own people and struck fear into the settlers.

Eventually it was two Aboriginal trackers who helped the police thwart Jundamurra's ambush at Six Mile Creek. He was wounded in the encounter and the police tracked him down and eventually shot him in the back.

Mulla Abdulla

Since 1788 Australians have only fought one battle on Australian soil. The invaders were two Afghanis — a butcher, Mulla Abdulla, who was also an imam at the Broken Hill mosque, and an ice-

The Bad — Politicians, Frauds, Hoaxers and Imposters

cream vendor named Gool Mohamed. Abdulla, age sixty, had been in trouble with the police for slaughtering sheep without a union card — no doubt he was butchering halal meat. According to a report by the ABC, the pair was known to smoke Indian hemp together and it was during one of these sessions that they hatched their plan.

The *Barrier Miner* reported that 'Mulla Abdulla had been sixteen years in Broken Hill, chiefly camel-driving. For the past few years he had been butcher for the camp at North Broken Hill, vested with priest rights in order to kill according to the Mohammedan religion. He was of a very reserved disposition, rarely speaking to anyone, and even the men in the camp are not sure where he was born. He was always childish and simple in his ways. He was unable to pay a fine when he was convicted for killing a sheep on unlicensed premises and has become very broody as a result. About this time Gool Mahomed came to the camp, and lived next to Abdulla. They became friends.'

On New Year's Day 1915, the Manchester Unity Order of Oddfellows Broken Hill branch set off by train for its annual picnic at Silverton. There were approximately 1200 men, women and children on board when, about two miles from Broken Hill, the train came under fire. Two people on board were killed and seven wounded.

The picnic was cancelled and the local police and military notified. The Afghanis — who had taken up arms in support of the Ottoman Empire — approached Broken Hill town. One man was shot in his house. The police were engaged near the Cable Hotel in Broken Hill and one policeman was shot before the police retreated and the Afghanis fell back to their home at the West Camel camp. They sensibly sought higher ground.

A battle ensued, lasting approximately an hour and a half, during which time Abdulla was killed and Mahomed wounded. A local, Jim Craig, was also killed after he refused to take cover.

The *Barrier Miner* reported that, 'In the battle there was a desperate determination to leave no work for the hangman, or to run the risk of the murderers of peaceful citizens being allowed to escape. It was not a long battle. The attacking party was being constantly reinforced by eager men, who arrived in any vehicles they could obtain or on foot. At just about one o'clock a rush took place to the Turks stronghold, and they were found lying on the ground behind their shelter. Both had many wounds. One was dead, the other expired at the Hospital later. They were in the dress of their people, with turbans on their heads. The police took charge of the bodies.'

Mohamed was taken alive but the sixteen bullet wounds he carried killed him shortly after reaching the hospital.

The battle was reported somewhat differently in Turkey ,where one newspaper wrote: 'We are pleased to report the success of our arms at Broken Hill, a seaport town on the west coast of Australia. A party of troops fired on Australian troops being transported to the front by rail. The enemy lost 40 killed and 70 injured. The total loss of Turks was two dead. The capture of Broken Hill leads the way to Canberra, the strongly fortified capital of Australia.'

Tempers were naturally inflamed as a consequence of the ambush. The local German population was blamed and the German Club was torched. A group of citizens also attempted to take revenge on the Afghan camel drivers in the area.

The police believed that Mohamed was the instigator of the attack. Somewhat malcontent, he used Abdulla's paranoia over his recent conviction to incite him to holy war — at least if he was dead he would go to heaven.'

The bodies were offered to the local Muslim community for burial but the Muslims refused to bury the pair on religious grounds, on the basis that they had disgraced their community.

Henry James O'Farrell

The first royal visit to Australia did not go well. Prince Alfred, Duke of Edinburgh, arrived for a tour in 1868. On 12 March the duke attended a function in his honour at Clontarf Beach and it was there that he was shot by Henry James O'Farrrell in Australia's first major assassination attempt.

Born in Dublin in 1833, O'Farrell had initially been called to religious orders. Just prior to ordination he abandoned the church for the land. He tried his hand at business and came to Australia. Things did not go well and he took to drink, which exacerbated his mental problems. He had a breakdown in 1867.

The following year his insanity intensified and that led to the shooting of the duke, who was not seriously injured. When arrested, O'Farrell claimed to have been overcome by the wrongs done to Ireland by the English.

Colonial Secretary Henry Parkes jumped into the public outrage. He declared that O'Farrell was a member of the Fenian Brotherhood, the precursors of the IRA, and immediately set up a task force to root out Irish sympathisers in the colony and put an end to incipient terrorism. The tensions between Protestants and Catholics intensified. The Legislative Assembly passed the *Treason Felony Act*, which made it an offence to refuse to toast the Queen.

Parkes rode the anti-Catholic tide, stirring up Protestant support. With that support he was able to introduce the *Public Instruction Act*, which abolished state aid for Catholic schools.

O'Farrell was quickly tried and hanged — against the wishes of the duke, who could see the man was insane — on 21 April 1898.

Public feeling ran high. There was a sens e of national embarrassment — the *Sydney Morning Herald* blamed it all on Victoria; public rallies of up to 20 000 people were held to show support for the Crown. A public subscription was taken up and its funds used to build Royal Prince Alfred Hospital in Sydney, 'to raise a permanent and substantial monument in testimony of the heartfelt gratitude of the community at the recovery of HRH'.

Jessie Street

Jessie Street was never a communist, although her enemies branded her 'Red Jessie' and considered her an enemy of the state. She was under constant surveillance by more than one intelligence service and that she was denied many government posts.

In fact, Jessie Street accomplished more international social reform than any of her contemporaries at a time when women were still supposed to be chained to the stove. She was born in India in 1889 and grew up in northern New South Wales on the Clarence River. Educated in Sydney and London, she graduated from Sydney University in 1912. After marrying Kenneth Whistler Street she could have settled for a comfortable life as a barrister's wife, but that was not her fate: the previous year she had attended a conference of the International Council for Women in Rome.

The women's suffrage movement was in full swing. Although most white women in Australia had the vote, there was certainly no economic or social equality between the sexes. Street was a vigorous campaigner for greater equality in the workplace. She founded the United Associations of Women. Street also attended international conferences including a delegation to the League of Nations in 1930 and was active with a number of international organisations, such as the International Labour Organization, pursuing equal rights for women. Street's pursuit of equal pay often led her into clashes with labour organisations and trade unions. In the 1940s, she campaigned for 'maintenance' to be paid to a mother who had left her husband and for an acknowledgement that a father should support his wife and child, but she did not win that fight. In 1933 she helped establish the first contraceptive planning clinic in Australia, to allow women some control over their fertility.

On a visit to Russia in 1938 Street was impressed by the equality between the sexes in the workforce. On the same trip she visited Germany and saw the effects of the Nazi race policies. The following year she joined the ALP. In 1943 she stood as the ALP candidate for the blue ribbon Liberal seat of Wentworth and was the first and only ALP candidate to win a majority of first preference votes in the seat.

Street had a great affection for the Soviet Union. During the Second World War she organised committees of friendship between Australia and Russia and, famouslym the 'Sheepskins for Russia' campaign.

In 1948 she was the only Australian woman delegate to the United Nations Conference on International Organization, held in San Francisco. There she helped draft the UN Charter and included the word 'sex' in the clause 'without distinction as to race, sex, language or religion'. She was co-founder of the UN Commission of the Status of Women and helped draft the Charter of women's rights. On her way home to Australia in 1949 she visited Hiroshima in Japan and was profoundly disturbed by the effect of the atomic bomb that had been unleashed by the Americans. At that point she became an even more determined campaigner for peace.

The Bad — Politicians, Frauds, Hoaxers and Imposters

Her following years were spent mostly in England, where she worked on a number of causes. Then in 1956 she returned to Australia and became involved in the civil rights struggle for Australian Aborigines. She co-drafted an amendment to the Australian Constitution to extend citizenship rights to Aborigines. She campaigned alongside prominent Aboriginal activists for civil rights up until the 1967 referendum, which amended the Constitution along the lines of her draft ten years earlier.

Street also found time for marriage and four children. Her husband became Chief Justice of New South Wales, as did her son Sir Lawrence. Jessie Street died in Sydney in 1970.

Jim Cairns

It's hard to believe that Jim Cairns was once a contender to lead the ALP. It's hard to believe that he was ever the spiritual leader of the Australian Left. Cairns did more damage to Australian post-war public life than any other individual and he will be remembered as the most juvenile public figure of the last century.

Jim Cairns' parents met on the boat as they emigrated to Australia in 1913 and their only child was born in October of the following year. Shortly after his son's birth, Jim Cairns Sr went to France to fight in the Great War. He never returned, abandoning his family and eventually settling in Kenya. The young Jim's mother worked as a cook and in service. Cairns grew up on a small farm at

Sunbury, Victoria, with his mother's extended family. His mother had contracted syphilis from his father and she was terrified of infecting her child, so there was no physical contact between mother and son.

On leaving school Cairns joined the police force and, after the outbreak of war, the army. Following his demobilisation, Cairns — by then a socialist — enrolled at Melbourne University, where he read economics. He then earned a scholarship to Oxford, where he also read economics. On returning to Australia, Cairns worked as an academic and author. He drifted into politics and, at the 1955 poll won the federal seat of Yarra.

Cairns was on the radical left of the ALP but he was one of the few to have academic and economic credentials. He became a key figure in the anti-Vietnam movement, and his abilities as a speaker also placed him high in the public perception. In 1968 he challenged Gough Whitlam for the ALP parliamentary leadership and lost only narrowly. However, in 1970 he had his finest moment, leading more than 100 000 protestors through the streets of Melbourne in the Vietnam Moratorium march.

After the 1972 ALP victory, Cairns was rewarded with the portfolio of Overseas Trade. In 1974 he became Treasurer. By that time a hike in wages and a spike in oil prices had sent inflation out of control. Cairns and his boss, Gough Whitlam, had lost control of the economy, but Cairns found time to begin an affair with his principal private secretary, Junie Morosi, which became common knowledge and a major scandal. Morosi was generally disliked by the press and loathed by the department over which she now exercised considerable power. Cairns exacerbated the matter at the national ALP conference in early 1975 by declaring to *The Sun* newspaper that he had 'a kind of love' for Morosi. The scandal greatly fuelled the disrepute the government had fallen into and made its loss at the next election almost a foregone conclusion.

The Morosi scandal had other, more damaging consequences. Morosi had been associated with Attorney-General Lionel Murphy, and the heat of her affair with Cairns meant that Whitlam had to postpone appointing Murphy to the High Court in late 1974. Had he appointed Murphy then it's likely that NSW Premier Tom Lewis would have followed precedent and filled the Senate vacancy with an ALP appointee. However, the Morosi scandal emboldened Lewis to defy precedent and appoint one of his own. A few months later, on the death of Senator Millner, Queensland Premier Joh Bjelke-Petersen followed Lewis's lead and the ALP lost its Senate majority. The stage was then set for Malcolm Fraser to block supply and have the Whitlam government dismissed.

Cairns was sacked in 1975 when he lied to Parliament. Shortly thereafter the ALP government collapsed. Cairns was not the sole architect of the destruction of the Whitlam government but he certainly played a major role.

After 1975 Cairns really made a fool of himself. He embraced the New Age and became a pensioner hippy, selling his books of New Age mumbo-jumbo on card tables at fairs and festivals. His major source of income was a defamation suit against the newspaper *The National Times*, which had suggested that a sexual relationship had occurred between Cairns and Morosi. Cairns denied the report and sued for libel. He won the action by perjuring himself in court and took the money. Shortly before his death in 2003 he admitted that he and Morosi had had an affair. He didn't return the money.

John Gorton

John Gorton was the most maverick of prime ministers. As a schoolboy he had shared a dormitory with Errol Flynn and if a prime minister could swashbuckle, then Gorton came close. Born in 1911 as the illegitimate son of a somewhat maverick businessman, Gorton was described by a journalist Alan Reid as a 'bustard' Gorton shot back: 'While I had that status thrust upon me by my parents, many people believed that Reid had earned the title by accepting the riding instructions of Sir Frank Packer.'

Gorton's legacy from his father was an orchard and small holding; it was enough to get him to Oxford, where he was studying at the outbreak of the Second World War. He subsequently enlisted in the Royal Australian Air Force, was shot down over Singapore and suffered terrible injuries. His face had to be almost completely reconstructed.

After the war Gorton returned to his orchard. He developed an interest in politics on the far right — virulently anti-Communist and pro–White Australia. In 1949 Gorton was elected to the Senate. Without realising it, he represented a new style of Australian politics: while conservative, he was also nationalistic; he was more American in his attitudes and had little time for the pomp and ceremony and anglophilia of Prime Minister Robert Menzies and the men of that era.

Gorton was an able senator and junior minister who didn't display much ambition. However, when Menzies's successor Harold Holt drowned at Christmas 1967, Gorton was unexpectedly parachuted into the top job. The leader of the Country Party, Jack McEwen, refused to serve in a government with Holt's logical heir, Treasurer and Deputy Billy McMahon — Gorton was the compromise candidate. He was given a safe lower house seat and became prime minister in early 1968.

'Jolly John, as we called him in Canberra almost from day one, made it quite clear that he wasn't going to be a conventional politician,' wrote journalist Mungo Macallum. 'He wasn't going to wear three-piece suits, and stay absolutely sober twenty-four hours a day, and never cock his eye when a good-looking woman went past. I mean, that wasn't Gorton's way.

'He was the first modern post-war Prime Minister — the one who shaped the change of direction. Whitlam, of course, built on it, during Whitlam's brief three years in office, but without Gorton having laid the foundations, Whitlam would've found it very much harder. I think that's really Gorton's legacy. He was the first of the new breed.'

The Liberal–Country Party coalition didn't know what hit them. Gorton was unconventional in his views; he was a modern thinker who wanted Australia to wake up from the torpor of the Menzies era. He was outspoken on many issues, informal and unconventional in his approach to ceremony and to policy.

Gorton's private life was also on display. There were rumours of affairs with his secretary Aynsley Gotto and of a dalliance with Liza Minnelli. Certainly he listened to her views and at that time the idea of a prime minister consulting a woman was outrageous. In one famous incident Gorton arrived drunk and late at the home of the American ambassador, in the company of a young woman journalist. He was heard to loudly criticise American policy in Vietnam and wish that he could withdraw Australian troops. Following the leaking of the events of the evening the Member for Warringah, Ted St John, called for Gorton's resignation.

Gorton also had no time for the Liberal state premiers and didn't disguise his contempt for them.

His lasting achievement was the establishment of the Australian film industry.

Although Gorton was personally liked by most Australians, the Liberals were under pressure from a resurgent ALP at the 1969 election and lost seats. The Liberals had been in office for almost two decades and it couldn't last. Ambitious ministers like Malcolm Fraser destabilised Gorton's administration and when McEwen died in 1971, McMahon made his move. Gorton resigned in March 1971 and the following year the ALP won government.

George Reid

Reid the Wriggler, an 'opportunist of the rankest kind' is how George Reid was described — even by his friends

Perhaps it's a tribute to his political opportunism that George Reid is the only politician to have been elected to the NSW state Parliament, the federal Parliament and the House of Commons.

Reid's career began unassumingly as a thirteen-year old clerk. He read law at Sydney University and was admitted to the Bar. He soon became immersed in the politics of New South Wales, where he was an avid free trader. Elected to the state seat of East Sydney in 1880, he rose to become premier. The issue of the day was Federation and Reid famously supported both the pro and anti causes, earning him the nickname 'Yes-No Reid'. Regardless, Reid's legacy in New South Wales can be seen in free compulsory education and the conciliation and arbitration system.

Reid was something of a bon vivant. His size was legendary; it was said that he did not walk — he rolled. WG McMinn described him as '[a]n almost ludicrously obese figure with a swaying pigeon-toed gait and a tendency to help himself along on the furniture, constantly popping sweets into his mouth, peering with the aid of a monocle over a great walrus moustache ... His appearance, his supposed public somnolence, his unattractive, high-pitched voice, the wit which was at its best when squashing an opponent or an interjector, seemed to more delicate souls to epitomise coarseness of mind and spirit.'

For all that, however, Reid also had a reputation as a ladies' man. Henry Parkes said of one woman that she must be of good character because neither he nor George Reid knew her.

The first Parliaments sat in Melbourne, a long way from Reid's barrister's chambers in Sydney. Both before and after his eleven-month tenure as Australia's fourth prime minister (August 1904 to July 1905) he found it hard to make the time to stay away from work and sit in Parliament, let alone leading a vigorous opposition. When in the Parliament he had a reputation for dozing off.

In 1910 he became Australia's first High Commissioner to London, where he put his social skills to good use. In 1916 he was offered the safe Commons seat of St George's Hanover Square two years before his death.

Reid's opportunism or pragmatism made him a controversial figure. According to writer Leonard Biggs, 'I remember how amazed I was that so fat a man with three fair, white chins of fascinating proportions could be so nimble witted and how startled I was by his squeaky, high-pitched voice. His capacity for sleep at any hour, in any place and in any circumstances was an asset which won the envy of us all.'

Joh Bjelke-Petersen

Born in New Zealand in 1911, Joh Bjelke-Petersen was still a small child when his family moved to Queensland, settling outside

The Bad — Politicians, Frauds, Hoaxers and Imposters

Kingaroy. Joh was brought up a God-fearing, hard-working farmer and he built the family holdings into a substantial operation.

In 1947 Bjelke-Petersen stood for the Country Party in the state seat of Nanango. While always committed to the interests of Queensland, Bjelke-Petersen saw public life as an opportunity to line his own pockets.

As early as 1957 he was parlaying influence with ministerial friends to secure mining leases and reap vast profits from them — in breach of the terms under which they were issued. His margin was some thousands of a per cent and he refused to pay tax on it.

When he became premier of Queensland in 1968, Bjelke-Petersen granted oil leases to two companies in which he had shares. The practice of selling political influence for cash continued until he left office. There were dozens of similar conflicts of interest that benefited the premier's bank account.

Alan Bond, then proprietor of the Nine Network, was sued by Bjelke-Petersen for defamation; he received a settlement of $400 000 cash that Bond said was the cost of doing business in Queensland.

A Singapore entrepreneur, Robert Sng, had a number of meetings with Bjelke-Petersen in the mid-1980s. At one of these, in September 1986, the Premier accepted $100 000 in cash in a brown envelope. When this transaction became the subject of a perjury charge, the premier escaped conviction. The jury was hung by one vote from a National Party supporter and the government demurred on a retrial on the basis of Bjelke-Petersen's health.

Due to the peculiarities of the electoral system in Queensland, it was possible for the National Party to rule the state even though they never achieved more than 40 per cent of the vote. As premier Bjelke-Petersen imposed an ultra-right agenda, using the police force as an arm of government and imposing dramatic restrictions on the freedom of speech and the freedom of assembly. Street marches protesting the government's policies were banned and citizens could be arrested for assembling in groups of more than three at a time. In 1971 he declared a state of emergency to prevent anti-apartheid marches during the South African rugby union team's tour.

Then in 1975 Bjelke-Petersen tore up the constitutional convention of replacing a deceased senator with a senator from the same party when he instituted a National Party senator as a replacement for an ALP senator, thus ending the Whitlam Government's Senate majority and setting the stage for the dismissal of Gough Whitlam as prime minister.

Now a player on the national stage, Bjelke-Petersen recognised few bounds. The police were strengthened and given their head — especially when prosecuting political dissenters. Corruption at all levels of the government was unabated. Against the advice of the straight-shooting Police Commissioner Ray Whitrod, in 1976 Bjelke-Petersen appointed Terry Lewis Commission. Lewis would later face a jail term of fourteen years for his corrupt behaviour.

ABC journalist Chris Masters uncovered the dark heart of Queensland with a *Four Corners* program titled 'Moonlight State'.

The Bad — Politicians, Frauds, Hoaxers and Imposters

The revelations of vice and corruption were so powerful that in May 1987 acting Queensland premier Bill Gunn set up a commission of inquiry eventually headed by Tony Fitzgerald QC. The Fitzgerald Inquiry was one of the most exhaustive and effective investigations in the nation's history.

Some 250 people were charged following the Fitzgerald inquiry, including three of Bjelke-Petersen's ministers: Geoffrey Muntz, Leisha Harvey and Russell Hinze. Lewis, whom the premier had recommended for a knighthood, was stripped of the title (the fourteenth person so divested in 700 years) and was jailed for fourteen years.

The Fitzgerald Inquiry was the end of Joh. He attempted to sack ministers who were a threat to him and tried a number of ruses to hold on to power but the state was too rotten and he had to go.

In December 1987, Joh Bjelke-Petersen retired.

Out of power he was now fair game, and he faced bribery and corruption charges. In each case the trials never came to fruition — although he was not acquitted either.

A Queensland jury in a 1992 defamation trial found that industrialist Sir Leslie Thiess had bribed Bjelke-Petersen from 1981 to 1984 generally 'on a large scale and on many occasions' — specifically, to procure government contracts involving Winchester South, Expo '88, a Gold Coast cultural centre and three prisons.' The Australian Broadcasting Tribunal also found that Bjelke-Petersen had extorted money from Alan Bond.

Queensland historian Ross Fitzgerald told the ABC shortly after Bjelke-Petersen's death in 2005: 'As I said when he was alive, it wouldn't matter if he lived to 137, it's very important not to forget that apart from being Queensland's longest-serving premier, he ran a corrupt and vicious regime that blighted the lives of tens of thousands of people, not just Aborigines and Islanders, not just civil libertarians, not just trade unionists — many of whom lost their jobs and superannuation in the SEQEB dispute, for example — but ordinary citizens who had the temerity to oppose his regime.

'You have got to remember that the Bjelke-Petersen regime involved the politicisation of the police force, so the police force was an arm of government. There was a very active Special Branch with a whole network of paid and unpaid informants that were in all the universities, in the ABC, in all the newspapers. Some of these informants were paid, some of them were unpaid. This ruined the careers of many people. It's important to remember at the time of Bjelke-Petersen, people were set up on all sorts of charges. People were set up on drug charges, drink-driving charges, and indecent exposure charges.

'The police force saw itself as an arm of government and the government saw the police as an arm of itself.'

In 1986, Clive James asked Bjelke-Petersen, 'Are you a fascist dictator?'

Joh replied, 'Some people say I am, Clive, but I think I'm a loving, kind one.'

The Bad — Politicians, Frauds, Hoaxers and Imposters

John Kerr

Australia's only famous governor-general stepped into history on 11 November 1975. The Queen's representative in Australia is never selected in the expectation that they will play a hand in domestic politics, but John Kerr decided to break the mould. Few governors-general get the opportunity to play their part, but Kerr jumped at the chance. The spring of 1975 was an extraordinary time in Australian politics and Kerr was the wrong man of the hour.

John Kerr was born in 1914 into a working-class family in the Sydney suburb of Balmain. He was a talented student who read law at the University of Sydney on a scholarship and was called to the New South Wales Bar in 1938. Kerr was considered one of the outstanding lawyers in the industrial relations courts, so, when required to find a successor to Governor-General Sir Paul Hasluck, Prime Minister Gough Whitlam appointed Kerr. Unfortunately, Whitlam did not appreciate the strength of either Kerr's alcoholism or his ego — and neither of these factors are generally relevant to the duties of the monarch's representative in Australia. As the governor-general is appointed by the Queen on the advice of the Prime Minister of the day, Whitlam assumed that if there was going to be any trouble he could just replace the governor-general. But he misjudged Kerr, believing him to be loyal to the consitutional conventions of the day.

In the winter of 1975 the Liberal Party leader Malcolm Fraser was determined to use his party's control of the Senate to unseat the ALP.

There is a constitutional convention which dictates that the parties respect the wishes of the voters at the previous election. However, the Liberal–Country Party coalition had defied those conventions in appointments to the Senate thus giving the conservatives a majority that had not been won at the 1974 election. There is a further convention that the upper house does not refuse the government of the day 'supply' — the taxation income it needs to run the country. The Liberals' lead in the polls meant that the opportunistic Fraser was determined to gain government by any means.

The Whitlam Government introduced its budget and the Senate blocked it. An already divided country was further split by a constitutional crisis. Whitlam intended to tough it out and there is evidence that he would have succeeded. However, Kerr— as opportunistic as Fraser — saw his moment. On 11 November 1975 he sacked Whitlam and asked Fraser to form a government.

Kerr recalled the day thus: 'I was sitting that morning for Clifton Pugh, who was painting my portrait. The door opened a little and Dave [Sir David Smith, Official Secretary] motioned to me to come back to my study. The execution warrant was ready for me to sign for that feller Whitlam'.

Even most Coalition supporters thought that Kerr had acted improperly. Kerr was a lightning rod for protest and certainly fuelled republican sentiment. But Fraser won the next election and Kerr remained in his post, although Kerr's drinking increased to the point where he was almost paralytic at the Melbourne Cup in 1977. Dressed in his favourite top hat and tails, he was victim of ridicule. Shortly thereafter he slunk off to a cushy retirement in Europe, where he could not embarrass Fraser further.

Sir Robert Askin

The former New South Wales Premier Sir Robert Askin was the chief architect of corruption in the state in the 1970s. He personally handed control of law and order over to corrupt police and their criminal partners, then he took a cut off the top.

Robert Askin was born as Robin Askin in 1907 and grew up in a working-class family in the Sydney suburb of Glebe. In the 1930s he ran an SP bookmaking operation. He then joined the Rural Bank and after World War II gravitated towards NSW politics. He entered the NSW Parliament in 1950 and was leader of the Liberal Party nine years later. A tough operator, he became premier in 1965.

According to writer David Hickie, 'Crime historians mark 1965 as the turning point in the development of organised crime in Australia, and especially New South Wales. As a former SP himself Askin identified this criminal network as a great source of political funds and support as well as personal goldmine.'

Askin and police commissioners Norman Allen and Fred Hanson reorganised the vice industry. They identified and then collected from the vast network of SP bookmakers, regulated the illegal casinos around Sydney and ensured that every major criminal paid protection money on a regular basis. In short, they institutionalised corruption. Askin received as much as $100 000 per year from gambler Perce Galea alone.

There was also a brisk trade for knighthoods, which could be had for between $60 000 until Buckingham Palace told the state government to stop asking for them.

Vladmir Petrov

On 3 April 1954, Vladimir Petrov defected to Australia. He was a KGB lieutenant colonel and his wife, Evdokia, was a KGB captain who specialised in codes. They had arrived in Australia in 1951 and fitted in reasonably well. Following Stalin's death in March 1953, Petrov feared that he would be purged or, at the least, have his meagre work appraised. He was instead cultivated by Australian spies who wanted to secure his defection.

It seems that Petrov's decision was not easily made: He didn't tell his wife of his plans and one day simply slipped into the arms of the Australians, who gave him £5000 and put him in a safe house. It was nine days before Petrov's defection was announced. Almost immediately afterwards Prime Minister Robert Menzies called a general election. Fear of the Communist menace was running high at the time and the Petrov Affair made it appear as though Australia was indeed being infiltrated by Soviet agents.

The Russians responded by wrapping themselves around Petrov's wife. It's not known how she felt about the defection, but on 19

April two KGB agents came to Australia to escort Evdokia back to Russia. When she lost her shoe on the tarmac at Sydney airport, the KGB agents dragged her onto the plane — a nice picture for the papers. The plane stopped in Darwin to refuel and it was here, over the course of a few nail-biting hours, that ASIO agents managed to get Mrs Petrov away from the Russians and convince her to defect.

Little was known of the Petrovs' work and little came out of their defection. However, the affair was useful because it gave the impression of a communist conspiracy in Australia and linked that conspiracy to the ALP. The less Petrov said publicly, the better it was for Menzies.

The royal commission and subsequent investigations into the Petrov Affair revealed that between 1945 and 1948 the KGB had two spies operating inside the Department of External Affairs. Petrov infiltrated some anti-Soviet groups, particularly in groups of migrants from the USSR and the Baltic States. In the end, however, his results had not been astounding. Vladimir Petrov went into hiding as Sven Allyson and his identity was protected until he and his wife died in 1991 and 2002 respectively. Like much of the Cold War, the reality of the Petrovs was far less sinister than their myth.

Billy Wentworth

Known as Bill or Billy, the great-grandson of the explorer William Charles Wentworth was a highly original character in the national public life.

According to Keith Dunstan in his book *Ratbags*, Billy Wentworth read Classic Mods at Oxford before returning to Australia to take up a menial position with Lever Brothers. He was soon edging towards Parliament when he became secretary to the New South Wales Attorney-General. Even in the 1930s, the defence of Australia was a passionate interest andjust before the outbreak of World War II Wentworth published a book, *Demand for Defence*, which argued that Australia faced a great threat from Japan.

When war was declared Wentworth signed up; unfortunately his very poor eyesight confined him to home defence. However, he threw himself into the challenge as a captain of the 45th Battalion.

In 1942 Wentworth was charged with staging a mock attack on Sydney to assess the city's level of preparedness. Captain Wentworth had studied the tactics of the Japanese and instructed his squad of seventy men to come ashore using their own ingenuity and then to pass through army lines and meet at a prearranged rendezvous near Cronulla, in the southern suburbs of Sydney.

Once they met, the team stole two buses and an army vehicle. Putting on a Japanese accent, Wentworth called the fire brigade and told them of a blaze in Sylvania, also in Sydney's south. He called the police and reported that a brawl had broken out amongst servicemen at Oyster Bill's at Tom Ugly's Point further north. Then he rang the emergency services and said an invasion had occurred at Cronulla. Wentworth put copper rods on the railway lines and short circuited the trains running south, putting the railway out of action for a week.

The Bad — Politicians, Frauds, Hoaxers and Imposters

When the emergency services team arrived at Cronulla they were ambushed by Wentworth's party and taken prisoner. Wentworth then staged an attack on battalion headquarters. The colonel, in his pyjamas, was taken prisoner. The ammunition dump was marked as destroyed.

With commandeered army vehicles Wentworth then lead his force west and took out the ammunition depot at Liverpool.

The Battle of Cronulla was a complete victory for Wentworth and a total disaster for the army. And for his troubles Wentworth was retired from duty.

Wentworth was a vehement anti-communist. He stood for Parliament as an independent and failed; upon finding a berth in the Liberal Party he was elected the Member for Mackellar on Sydney's northern beaches — a post he held until 1977 — but he was not much liked by Robert Menzies or Harold Holt and remained on the backbench.

Wentworth did not sit quietly, however: he was a vocal and passionate advocate for a number of issues. After defence he took on that most thorny of issues — the railway gauge. It was through his passionate and relentless pursuit of the issue that the federal government finally agreed to a single-gauge track between Sydney and Melbourne and the train that became the Southern Aurora.

Wentworth was also an advocate for the rights of the poor and the indigenous. He supported the Gurindji claim at Wave Hill station and helped to start that long process towards acceptance of the claim for land rights by Aboriginal people.

Wentworth was elevated to the ministry under John Gorton, becoming the first Minister for Aboriginal Affairs. He had little stomach for his successors and remained a loose cannon in Parliament until his retirement.

Journalist Alan Reid described Wentworth well when he wrote, 'He is that unnerving mixture of prophet and demagogue and of eccentric and near genius.'

William Lane

Born working-class in England, William Lane became a journalist and a committed socialist. In 1883 he was in Queensland, working for the left-wing press. Lane was a very successful writer and an impressive advocate for trade unionism — he was instrumental in the formation of the Brisbane Trades and Labour Council. In 1887 he started his own newspaper, *The Boomerang*, and attracted contributors of the order of Henry Lawson to its pages. The paper was a considerable success in what was a very intense period for the Australian working man. The beginnings of the Labour movement came through significant periods of industrial unrest and were resisted sternly by the forces of capital.

Lane became increasingly committed to the ideal of a worker's paradise; he even wrote a novel with that title. Despairing of finding his paradise in Australia, however, he hatched a plan to build a communist community in the jungles of Paraguay.

The Bad — Politicians, Frauds, Hoaxers and Imposters

Land was found and an agreement reached with the Paraguay Government. The New Australia Co-operative Settlement Association was established with capital of £30 000. On 17 July 1893 the Association's boat, *The Royal Tar*, set sail from Sydney with 220 true believers on board. They arrived at Montevideo on 13 September and then, with another vessel, navigated the La Plata River, arriving at New Australia on 4 October.

Lane was the magistrate and the unquestioned leader of New Australia, where the citizens were guaranteed freedom of 'thought, religion, speech and leisure and in all matters whatsoever'. Property was communal and shared equally, as was domestic work.

Life in the commune was not easy: food was scarce and the jungle forever threatened the inhabitants' livelihoods. As things became tougher, Lane became more of a despot and the villagers were less inclined to follow his 'utopian' ideals. Lane expelled three men for getting drunk in a nearby village and tensions simmered. In March 1894 a new group of settlers arrived and factions grew.

Dispirited, Lane took forty-five adults further up the river and established the village of Cosme. The workers' paradise continued to attract interest from Australia, including from poet Mary Gilmore, who lived at Cosme for a time. But the same struggles with the jungles continued and food eventually all but ran out.

By sheer will, Lane established the village. Settlers continued to arrive and it was clear that the experiment would survive — but not thrive.

Establishing this community had been a huge effort for Lane and took its toll on his emotions, intellect and health. By 1899 Cosme had its own tram system, printing works, sugar mill, workshops and dining rooml however, in August 1899 he left, still faithful to the community but needing to care for his ill family. He went to New Zealand, where he once again took up journalism and was again a great success. Lane eventually succeeded to the post of editor of *The New Zealand Herald* and was still in that role when he died in 1917.

Although the leader of a quixotic crusade, Lane was universally respected a s a man of high moral fibre and great courage. After returning to New Zealand he never wrote of discussed his South American adventure.

The descendants of the first settlers are still living in Cosme and New Australia.

William Hughes

Born into a Welsh-English family, William Morris Hughes came to Australia in 1884. He had, according to his own account, a variety of jobs on the land: drover, swagman, boundary rider, factory hand, umbrella mender and railway fettler. He finally settled in Balmain, Sydney, opening a mixed business and marrying in 1890.

Hughes was a physically small man with a very large ego and a natural talent for public speaking. He gravitated towards the Left due to his natural affinity for the idea of struggle. In those years before Federation Hughes became active in the formation of the Australian Labour Party. He also found a home in the union movement, helping to found the Australian Workers' Union, and was the first president of the Waterside Workers' Federation. He was rewarded with a seat in the NSW Parliament in 1894.

In 1901 Hughes became the Member for West Sydney in the first federal pand was Attorney General in Andrew Fisher's Labor Cabinet.

In 1915 Billy Hughes became Australia's eleventh prime minister. The nation was at war and Hughes threw himself into the struggle. Massive casualties in the early stages of the war — notably at Gallipoli — required ever more manpower for the Imperial forces. But the war effort was not universally supported in Australia however. Cardinal Mannix, who led the Catholic Church in Australia at the time, was Irish and therefore anti-British. When Hughes tried to introduce conscription for overseas service, Mannix vigorously opposed the policy. The country was split, largely on sectarian lines. The Labor Party, with its large Catholic bloc, was also split.

In 1916 Hughes introduced a referendum on conscription and was defeated. He was so convinced on the issue that he quit the ALP and took with him sufficient defectors to form a new government as the National Labor Party.

In 1917 he was back out campaigning for a second referendum on the issue. In November 1717 he was in the Queensland town of Warwick when some protestors, including one Patrick Brosnan, pelted him with eggs. The Prime Minister demanded that the local policeman arrest the culprit but the Queensland police refused;

Hughes was furious. He attempted to carpet the Queensland premier Thomas Ryan, who also refused to act. In response Hughes establish what would become the Federal Police.

In any event, the second referendum was also lost.

At the end of the war Hughes attended the Paris Peace Conference, where he made quite a name for himself and for Australia. He insisted that Australia be represented not simply as an extension of Great Britain, and he secured control over New Guinea.

Hughes was immensely popular, especially with the servicemen who called him 'Little Digger', but he was also divisive. He won the 1919 election but by 1922 the coalition of Labor defectors, conservatives and the Country Party wanted a new, less-populist leader and he was replaced by Stanley Melbourne Bruce.

As a Labor rat Hughes was exiled to the conservative benches, although he was an aggressive player in Parliament. He helped to bring down Bruce in 1929 and was active in the United Australia Party until expelled and thence helped Robert Menzies found the Liberal Party.

Hughes remained in Parliament from the time he was first elected until he died as the member for Bradfield in 1952.

Jack Lang

Born the son of watchmaker, Jack Lang was a real estate agent until he joined the New South Wales Parliament in 1913. He had been

The Bad — Politicians, Frauds, Hoaxers and Imposters

born in 1896 and grew up in the Sydney suburb of Brickfield Hill. His *petite bourgeoisie* Catholic attitude was one of his defining characteristics, especially in his battles against the Communist Party. Known as 'the Big Fella', Lang was one of the most controversial politicians of his era.

Lang was Treasurer in the NSW Labor Government of 1920–21, and Premier and Treasurer of the State twice (1925–27 and 1930–32). Under his leadership in the first term a range of social welfare reforms were introduced: child endowment, widows' pensions, increased workers' compensation rates, the 44-hour week and the abolition of secondary school fees.

Under Lang's leadership the ALP was returned to power in 1930; by 1931 almost 450 000 Australians were out of work. The nation's finances — at the time completely dependent on those of Britain — were in dire straits. As premier of New South Wales, Lang proposed a policy of 'Australia First!'. Britain did not agree.

In 1930 the Bank of England appointed Sir Otto Niemeyer to solve its colonial problem. Niemeyer proposed a policy of cutting wages to make exports more competitive (at the time the country was locked into an almost exclusive trade relationship with Britain) and a widespread policy of austerity that meant the abolition of social welfare. Niemeyer wanted Australia to create immediate surpluses so that it could maintain its interest payments to Britain — the maintenance of cash flow back to the Mother Country was his sole objective.

The Bank of England's plan was called the Melbourne Agreement of August 1930 and the federal and state governments, with the exception of New South Wales, supported it.

Lang had his own plan. He believed that in times of crisis the government should use its resources to keep the money supply liquid and the economy buoyant. The prevailing wisdom was completely different — until the Depression deepened and the American economy failed to respond. Keeping the money supply liquid was turned into a theory by John Maynard Keynes and adopted by US President Franklin D Roosevelt as the New Deal. It saved the US and was the cornerstone of economy policy for the next forty-five years. Lang was not as sophisticated as Keynes but his instinct and intellect had told him which way to go.

Instead of cutting wage costs, Lang suspended payment to the UK and reduced interest on all government debts to Australians. He encouraged the orderly extension of credit by the banks and finally embarked on a large-scale expansion of public works, including the building of the Sydney Harbour Bridge.

Lang stirred up national spirit at public meetings with demands such as 'The same people who conscripted our sons and laid them in Flanders' fields … Now demand more blood, the interest on their lives …'

Conservatives were naturally inclined to believe that Australians should put Britain first; they barely recognised their Australian citizenship and certainly still regarded the nation as a colony. At worst they feared Lang was leading down the path of communism. Nothing could have been further from Lang's beliefs.

A group of citizens with a neofascist ideology formed what was known as the New Guard and received funding from large firms and banks. At its zenith the New Guard numbered almost 100 000 members. Its ranks were filled by ex-soldiers and small business people with strong affiliations to Britain. Many public meetings were held, and many public rallies became pitched battles of the New Guard versus the workers.

In 1931 the NSW ALP fell out with the Scullin ALP Government in Canberra over Niemeyer's plan. In Canberra five NSW representatives brought down the federal government. Scullin left the ALP and formed a new government while Lang led a breakaway section of the ALP known as Lang Labor.

Matters came to a head in 1932. Lang's crowning monument to public spending, the Sydney Harbour Bridge, was finished and ready for opening. Shortly before Lang could cut the ceremonial ribbon, a New Guardsman named Francis DeGroot came through with his sword out and cut it first.

Worse was to come.

Scullin made directions regarding the finances of New South Wales — Lang defied him and hung onto the money. On 13 May 1932 the NSW governor, Sir Philip Game, acted in the name of the King as he dismissed Premier Jack Lang and ordered new elections.

Lang was not returned. He eventually stood for federal parliament and held a seat until 1949. In 1941 he was formally expelled from the ALP and was only readmitted in 1971, four years before his death in 1975.

Despite his expulsion, Lang remained a Labor hero, especially to future prime minister Paul Keating, but also to republican Australians.

Eureka Stockade

As we all know, the British Government developed Australia as a place to put its troublemakers. A large number of them were Irish *and* Catholic and for the first 160 years of European settlement in Australia the British replicated a system that had proved flawed at home: sending the Irish to Australia under the supervision of Protestant English. To no one's surprise, surely, the Irish rebelled. The most famous uprising occurred at Ballarat in 1854.

The trouble started some years earlier, when the Victorian Parliament imposed fees on the 'diggers' on the goldfields. By 1852 these taxes had reached a painful £1 10/- a month. The diggers responded by saying that they had no representatives in Parliament to speak for them and, like the Americans in 1776, felt that there should be 'no taxation without representation'. The Parliament was generally dominated by the wealthy and the squatting class, and it had little respect for the Irish, the Chinamen and others of the working poor hoping for a windfall. Consequently, the police and the troopers were often brutal in their maintenance of order and the collection of fees.

The Bad — Politicians, Frauds, Hoaxers and Imposters

Matters came to a head on 6 October 1854 when a miner was killed at the Eureka Hotel in Ballarat. Others miners burned the hotel to the ground in the mistaken belief that the murderer was getting support from the authorities. It was simply the match to a tinderbox. When three diggers were arrested for arson, a large group of the others formed the Ballarat Reform League. They demanded not only their comrades' release but also the abolition of licences, the abolition of the proper qualification for Members of Parliament and the vote.

Now organised, the diggers made representations of their demands to the lieutenant governor. They were rebuffed, and so resolved to hold a public meeting on Wednesday, 29 November on Bakery Hill, at which their licences would be burned. Twelve thousand people turned up. Some were destroyed. The meeting resolved to boycott the licence system. The women hastily made a flag — the Southern Cross on a blue background — and it was run up the flagpole.

The following day the police again swooped on miners without licences. Word spread through the diggings and the miners rushed back to Bakery Hill, forcing the troopers and police to retreat. The Southern Cross flag was again raised and one Peter Lalor became unofficial spokesman. He urged his comrades to arm themselves in self-defence and declared, 'We swear by the Southern Cross to stand truly by each other to defend our rights and liberties'.

Lalor was born at Tinakill in Queen's County, Ireland, in 1827. Lalor's family had been fighting the English since the sixteenth century. His father, Patrick had been a rebel leader before he took up a seat in the House of Commons and his brother James was jailed for revolutionary activities. Lalor was educated at Carlow College. Dublin, and emigrated to Australia in 1852.

On 1 December Lalor began organising his force of some 1500 men on Bakery Hill, in what was to become known as the Eureka Stockade. Lalor wrote that the stockade was a makeshift affair built mostly for the purpose of keeping the rebels together in one place. His family's experience in armed uprisings came to the fore as he divided up the roles in the camp, preparing for an attack.

Then, on the morning of 3 December, 276 troopers stormed the 120 rebels inside the Eureka Stockade. The attack was a complete surprise. In the half-hour battle thirty rebels and four troopers died, and more than 100 diggers were arrested. Lalor injured his arm in a gun battle but he escaped the fighting and was taken in by sympathisers; his arm was later amputated. Governor Hotham placed a bounty of £200 on Lalor's head; nonetheless he remained hidden for some weeks and was eventually moved to his fiancée's house in Geelong. When he finally emerged in public he was not arrested. Most of the rebels, however, were eventually caught and tried but no jury would convict them. Hotham acceded to the diggers' demands for representation and two seats were created for Ballarat, one of which was won by Lalor.

As a parliamentarian Lalor was an unpredictable character. At first a vigilant supporter of diggers' rights, he was also a believer in creating a solid, land-owning middle class and many of his positions were quite conservative. Nonetheless, Lalor was eventually elected Speaker of the Victorian Legislative Assembly in 1880, a position he held until 1887 through a number of different administrations. He declined a knighthood and died in January 1889.

The Battle of Vinegar Hill

New South Wales was an aggregation of surly, seditious and mostly Irish convicts. The Irish were constrained on practicing the Mass — which was a serious issue for them. When however the administration relented and allowed Irish Catholics to congregate, they used the opportunity to formant rebellion.

The Battle of Vinegar Hill in County Wexford in 1798 saw dozens of Irish rebels transported to Australia. One Phillip Cunningham was among them. Cunningham and William Johnston planned to stage a rebellion in New South Wales and, if all went well, to capture some ships and make their way back to free Ireland.

The harsh conditions in the colony aided the recruitment of a sizeable number of convicts and Cunningham's experience as an agitator gave him the experience to organise an effective band and to enforce discipline in his troops. Cunningham was also an admirable tactician: he devised a plan to start fires on the north and west outskirts of the settlement to draw out the garrison westwards.

At 9 p.m. on the evening of 4 March 1804, John Cavenah set fire to his hut in Castle Hill to the northwest of Sydney Town. Due to a communication breakdown, the uprisings in Parramatta didn't start as planned. Nevertheless, Cunningham and Johnston's rebels ranged across the northwest of Sydney yelling the way cry 'Death of Liberty'. Cunningham then led 200 men into Government Farm, where they acquired swords, guns and ammunition. The Hills District flogger, Robert Duggan, was roused from under his bed and beaten senseless.

Stories of the rebellion spread even faster than the rebels. The Marsden and Macarthur families rightly considered themselves targets. Cunningham wanted to divert the Parramatta regiment by setting fire to the Macarthur estates while his troops rallied at Constitution Hill in Parramatta. Governor King declared martial law in Parramatta, Castle Hill, Toongabbie, Prospect, Seven and Baulkham Hills, Hawkesbury and Nepean.

Cunningham massed his troops at Constitution Hill, also known as Sugar Loaf Hill, and marched on Parramatta, looting along the way. They collected as many as a third of the colony's weapons by the time they reached Parramatta.

Back in Sydney, Major George Johnston gathered twenty-nine soldiers and made a very quick, disciplined overnight march to Parramatta. Meanwhile, the rebel forces began to lose focus. They lacked communication and experience, and by dawn their plan was in tatters.

Meanwhile, Johnston's force had almost caught up with the insurgents. The two forces met at Rouse Hill; Johnston met with Cunningham. The rebels thought there were negotiations to be had but Johnston was only playing for time until his line was reinforced.

The Bad — Politicians, Frauds, Hoaxers and Imposters

The leaders withdrew and then Cunningham and William Johnston rode to meet the army. They were immediately taken prisoner and the troopers attacked the rebels, who stood little chance in the half-hour battle.

According to historian Lynette Ramsey Silver: 'Major Johnston without any other preliminaries ordered his men to charge and open fire. Over fifty armed civilians, a mounted trooper, and 29 military men (26 of whom were capable of firing 780 prepared rounds of ammunition in 10 to 15 minutes), were pitted against 233 rebels. The odds were technically with the rebels, but it was Enniscorthy's Vinegar Hill all over again. With machine-like precision and the economy of movement that comes with practice and military training, the red-coated soldiers formed ranks and for 15 minutes carried out their duty precisely as ordered. Leaderless, caught completely unawares and totally unprepared, the rebels weakly returned the fire before fleeing in all directions.'

Cunningham, wounded in the initial affray, was summarily tried and hanged from a staircase outside a shop in Windsor. Some fifteen rebels were killed in the fighting that came to be known as the Battle of Vinegar Hill after the Irish rising.

'I think the reason why it should be commemorated is that for the first time in Australian history, there are some political issues put on the agenda by citizens — convicts, rebels, political prisoners,' said Jonathan King, an historian and descendant of Governor King. 'They said, "Hey, we want freedom. We want democracy. We want to practise our own culture, our own religion." That led through to self-government in the 1850s, after Eureka, and Federation. So those people who died were actually martyrs to a cause — the democratic cause that we enjoy today.'

'The results of Vinegar Hill were long delayed,' said Gough Whitlam in a 1988 speech dedicating a memorial to the Battle. 'It took a generation before Irish priests were freely allowed to officiate in New South Wales. After Ireland gained independence citizens of Ireland and UK were both automatically Australian citizens and compulsory Australian electors.

'The Bicentennial has concentrated our knowledge of Australian history. We now speculate on early Portuguese explorers, we acknowledge the history of the Aborigines; we shall rank Vinegar Hill with Eureka. We give equal honour to all the peoples who have come to Australia and will build its future.'

Thomas Ley

Australia has more than its fair share of corrupt politicians, but Thomas Ley takes the cake. As the New South Wales Minister for Justice, Ley was not known for his clemency. When capital cases were referred to him as the penultimate appeal for mercy, his view was invariably negative.

Ley was born at Bath in England in 1880, the son of a butler. His widowed mother brought the family of four children and their grandmother to Australia in 1886. Money was hard to come by. Ley

The Bad — Politicians, Frauds, Hoaxers and Imposters

was working while still a primary school student. and by the age of ten he had finished school and was working in the family store. Ambitious and hardworking, he took night classes and worked his way into a law firm. In 1914 he became a solicitor.

Ley had his eye on politics and in 1907 moved to Hurstville, where he was elected to the local council. He was very active in local affairs and especially the cause of prohibition, which earned him the sobriquet 'Lemonade Ley'. Unable to gain the mayoralty, he stood for the NSW Parliament and became was elected to the Legislative Assembly in 1917. He was not much liked by his colleagues. According to the *Australian Dictionary of Biography*, he was 'a "fluent speaker, with a most unctuous manner", and deluded many with his community work and pious utterances.' Or, in the words of Jack Lang, 'The greatest rogue. He inspired the most disgraceful sectarian campaign in the history of the State.'

Despite his prohibitionist supporters, Ley was capable of supporting the brewing interests. In 1922 he was appointed Minister of Justice and that period was most notable for Ley's refusal of clemency in a murder case, despite a loud public outcry.

With few friends in Macquarie Street, perhaps Ley thought federal politics was a fresh start. He stood for Barton in 1925 and, dubious about his electability, tried to bribe the sitting ALP member, Fred McDonald. When Ley won the seat, McDonald took the matter to the Court of Disputed Returns. Unfortunately McDonald disappeared in mysterious circumstances. Although he was never charged, suspicion descended on Ley.

Ley's business interests occupied some of his time, more so as they went bad. He was involved in schemes for oil and the prickly pear, both of which had their share of disgruntled investors. One partner, Hyman Goldstein, threatened to take Ley to court but somehow fell to his death on rocks in the beachside suburb of Coogee. Another investor, Keith Greedor, drowned.

The body count did little for Ley's electability and he was defeated in the 1928 ballot. At this point he left his wife and two children, and returned to England with his widowed mistress, Maggie Brooks (her husband had also died mysteriously). It was said that the prime minister encouraged Ley, now a wealth man, to make the move.

In England Ley was a con man and blackmarketeer. Love finally undid him. however, when he strangled John McBain Mudie, whom he thought to be having an affair with Brooks. Ley was sentenced to death — a punishment he had meted out with glee to others. Only days before his execution, the sentence was commuted and he was committed to Broadmoor Criminal Lunatic Asylum. He died there two months later, in 1947.

THE DANGEROUS — KILLERS, SERIAL AND OTHERWISE

Australia is still coming to terms with the first years of European settlement. Three themes which dominated the minds of the Botany Bay garrison — its geographical isolation, the relationship with the indigenous population and the harsh climate — have not yet been resolved.

Crime and its aftermath was clearly at the forefront of those issues. In many ways we are still dealing with all those characters — the psychopaths, the sociopaths, the professional crooks, the harsh judiciary.

In lieu of many other contenders, we have fallen back on bushrangers as the folk heroes of the Colonial period. Some of them, like Jimmy Governor, have in their stories important tales about the origin of the country and others, like Mad Dog Morgan, were simply men driven mad by the country.

Then there is Ned Kelly, perhaps our most famous Australian. Our greatest artists in literature, cinema and paint, have explored the Kelly story as one of our most profound myths. Kelly himself has been the most examined Australian historical figure. He remains an enigma behind an iron mask

— his Irish heritage, his revolutionary spirit, his ingenuity, his compassion or otherwise (there is much dispute on this) and his love for his mother. It's through the Kelly story that most of us know whatever it is about life in nineteenth century Australia.

The bushrangers gave way to the street gangs of the first half of the twentieth century. For most of that period the laws relating to gaming and liquor were opposite to the Australian identity of a knockabout larrikin. And so the peddlers of vice became folk heroes in a sense. In this section we have a selection of the better known — Squizzy Taylor the Melbourne hitman and Sydney's vice Queens Tilly Devine and Kate Leigh. In addition we have some smaller stories of those like Jean Lee and Nellie Cameron who were caught up in this world with tragic results. Again, it is through the stories of the fallen that we get a sense of working class life.

And so it goes on. The tradition that began with the bushrangers has continued in Melbourne with the recent 'Underbelly' gang wars and in Sydney with the 'Blue Murder' years.

Then there are the simply bad men and women — the psychopaths and sociopaths who have sent shivers through the community. Time has allowed us to come to terms with some of them such as the diabolical dentist of Wynyard Square. Others, like the Tasmanian cannibal Alexander Pearce, are in the process of becoming folk heroes in the future.

Alexander Pearce

There was no better poster boy for the brutality of the Tasmanian prison environment. Alexander Pearce, was born in Ireland in 1790. He was a hardened criminal by the time he was convicted in the County Armagh Lent Assizes of 1819 and transported to Van Dieman's Land via Sydney in 1821. His crime was the theft of six pairs of shoes.

Prison did not suit Pearce well. In his first six months in Tasmania he was flogged for stealing poultry, being drunk, stealing a wheelbarrow and absconding. The prisoners spent most of their time hewing Huon pine trees and hauling them for shipbuilding on Macquarie Harbour. On 20 September 1822, Pearce, Alexander Dalton, Thomas Bodenham, William Kennerly, Matthew Travers, Edward Brown, Robert Greenhill and John Mather devised a plan to overpower their overseer and make for the coast where a boat would be hijacked and they would sail to the Pacific or China. The plan went awry immediately and instead they struck off westward into the dense Tasmanian rainforest. In the early nineteenth century, settlements had been established on the east and west coasts but the centre of the island had not been explored. This was some of the most difficult, dense and perilous country to be encountered by Europeans. It was a wilderness in every sense of the word, They had no clear idea how they would reach the other side or when.

After eight days and on the verge of starvation it was decided to eat Alexander Dalton. There was a general agreement that Dalton, who had been a flogger, was the most deserving. There was a widely held law of the sea that cannibalism was acceptable in situations where a crew was on the verge of starvation and help unlikely in the near future. While there are no reliable examples of this course of action being taken, these were already desperate men in dire circumstances. Brown and Kennerly, fearing they were next, left the party and headed back but perished in the bush. The others went on. Food was hard to come by. They ate berries and boiled their kangaroo skin jackets but their hunger was not abated. One by one the escapees were eaten. Apparently human flesh is low in carbohydrate and not a good source of energy so that was the reason why cannibalism was never satisfying their hunger and why the had to kill regularly. No matter how much they ate of their companions they were always hungry, needing the strength to continue their journey.

Eventually it came down to just Greenhill and Pearce, and the former fell asleep first. After forty-two days, Pearce chanced upon a convict shepherd who took him in. He spent a few weeks robbing the locals and hanging about with some of them before being recaptured.

Pearce confessed all but was not believed. He was returned to Sarah Island near Hobart.

Two months later, Pearce and Thomas Cox escaped, this time heading northward. After only a few days a fight broke out and Pearce killed Cox. According to some reports, he was annoyed that Cox couldn't swim and was otherwise holding him up. There was the suggestion however, in Pearce's own account that Cox's primary function was culinary. Although he had other food available he butchered his companion and roasted his flesh — especially the thigh that he pronounced to his captors the best eating.

Peace was probably insane by the time he escaped from prison the second time. Certainly, the time he was recaptured he was at his wits' end. In desperation and remorse he made himself known to a passing ship and was once again recaptured. This time, he was believed and the body of Cox was discovered — dismembered and disembowelled. He was hanged on 19 July 1824.

The Gun Alley Murder

At 6 a.m. on 31 December 1921, in a Melbourne lane known as Gun Alley, Alma Tirtschke, twelve, was found dead — raped and strangled. The crime shocked Melbourne to its core. Alma had left her grandmother's house in Jolimont to collect meat from the butcher TK Bennet and Woolcock's of 154 Swanston Street in the city and then to deliver the package to her aunt in nearby Collins Street. She was a good student and a level-headed girl who was seen by several witnesses walking the streets of Melbourne on her errand, window-shopping on the way. She was last seen at 3 p.m., at the entrance to the Eastern Arcade.

Melbourne was up in arms about the case. The newspapers demanded results, chastising the police, who toiled for a fortnight unearthing no clues. The government quadrupled the reward for information to £1000 and the *Herald* offered a further £250. The pressure on police for a culprit was at fever pitch.

Then suddenly, in late January 1922, the police arrested Colin Campbell Ross, the keeper of a saloon in the Eastern Arcade near where Alma disappeared. This was a sleazy part of town, and Ross served drinks to shady characters. He was undoubtedly no angel, although he was not personally directly linked to any criminal activity or vice. Some of his former employees and clients — all of them small-time criminals — gave evidence against him. Once implicated in the crime, his house was raided. Police found a blanket which had, they said, Alma's hairs on it.

Ross had an alibi for most of the time in question but that did him no good. Not only did police have witnesses eager to share in the reward money, but also for the first time in Australia police used forensic evidence — strands of hair — to build their case.

The five-day trial began on 20 February 1922. From the beginning, Ross proclaimed his innocence. Few believed him. Ross was found guilty of murder and sentenced to be hanged. Colin Ross was executed at the old Melbourne Jail on 24 April 1922

Fatefully, the painter Charles Blackman was sufficiently disturbed by the case that he painted a series entitled 'Gun Alley'. Seventy years later, in 1993, librarian Kevin Morgan became haunted by the pictures and began his own investigation that led him to believe in Ross' innocence. He re-examined the case files and discovered that the police had withheld important information from the jury, including six reliable alibi witnesses.

By a stroke of luck the forensic evidence was still on file, and Morgan was able to get the hairs DNA-tested — proving conclusively that they did not come from the victim's head. Morgan's research proved that an innocent man had gone to the gallows for no reason other than to silence the braying of the tabloid press.

In May 2008, 86 years after he was hanged, Ross was granted a posthumous pardon — the first in Victoria's history.

George 'Possum' Dean

By all accounts, George 'Possum' Dean was one of the more popular young men of Sydney. He was born at Albury in 1867, the son of a miner of Irish extraction. At the age of twelve he was convicted of illegal use of a horse. Unable to pay the £5 fine, he spent a short time in Wagga Wagga Jail.

All that was behind him by 1884 when he took up a position with the North Shore Steam Ferry Co. and gained his Master's Certificate four years later. He was the night shift captain of a ferry which steamed between Circular Quay and Milson's Point. Dean had some four times jumped into the Harbour to rescue women who had fallen overboard. George Dean was a good-looking young man of twenty-seven when he fell in love with Mary Seymour.

They were the picture of the perfect couple, setting up house together in Miller Street, North Sydney. Within a year they had their first child. The one fly in the ointment was Mary's mother.

Mrs Seymour owned a fruit shop at 411 Riley Street, Surry Hills. She had a questionable background having arrived in Australia as a convict. She was the veteran of a number of marriages and Mary had been born illegitimate while her father was in Pentridge Prison.

It was all too much for Dean. As he grew to know the family he suspected that the women might have conspired to seduce him to profit from his money and his good name.

Dean resolved that the only way out was to get rid of his wife. He began by adding arsenic and strychnine to Mary's favourite treat — lemon syrup. He also added the poison to her tea and to her beef tea.

Mary became concerned about the bitter taste of the liquids her husband was preparing for her so she kept some aside and had it analysed. When she discovered poison the police were called. On 19 March 1895 — George Dean appeared at the Court of Petty Sessions, North Sydney, charged with administering poison to his wife, with intent to kill her.

A routine police case was somewhat complicated by the legal prowess of Richard Meagher, counsel for the defence. In association with his friend and colleague William Crick, Meagher dragged the background of Mrs Seymour through the courts and impugned the virtue of Mary Dean. They implied that the whole thing was a plot by these two women to get rid of Dean.

The judge, William Windeyer was a severe jurist who thought Dean clearly guilty and there is some suggestion that he leaned on the jury to deliver that verdict.

The Dangerous — Killers, Serial and Otherwise

Dean was convicted and Windeyer had no hesitation in pronouncing the death sentence.

The public, whipped up by the press, were outraged. Here was a hero being brought down by scheming whores. The outcry was so great that the government was obliged to call a Royal Commission. The first of its kind in the Colony.

The Royal Commission heard that Mrs Seymour was a procuress and brothel keeper. The police said that she was one of the best pickpockets in the Colony. An enormous amount of evidence was given on all sides. At the end the Commissioners overturned the original verdict and freed Dean.

The ferryman was now a celebrity. People came from all over town to ride on the boats he captained.

All would have been well except that Richard Meagher wanted to run for Parliament. The *Daily Telegraph* published a story that implied that Meagher had not been a good enough advocate to win the Dean case. The lawyer's pride was dented and he intended to sue the paper for libel. He consulted his colleague Sir Julian Salomon and explained that he was a good enough lawyer as to have successfully defended Dean whom he knew was guilty.

Meagher had tricked Dean into a confession. The ferryman had gotten the arsenic from a chemist RJ Smith as a gift. All of the chemists in Sydney were questioned as to whether they had sold Dean the arsenic. Meagher was careful in his examination of Smith to ask whether he had 'sold' the poison. To which Smith had truthfully answered 'no'.

Salomon was in the invidious position now of having a confidence from a colleague and knowing that to keep it would pervert justice. In the end, he followed his conscience. He told the Attorney-General.

Dean had been pardoned of the murder of his wife and couldn't be retried. He was charged with making false statements and perverting the course of justice for which he received fourteen years.

Meagher was struck off the rolls as a solicitor. It took him another twenty years to get back on. In the meantime he sat in the NSW Parliament and held high offices in the ALP, including the first Labor Lord Mayor of Sydney.

George Dean was released from prison in 1904. By this time, Mary had remarried and George went back to his old position on the ferries By the outbreak of the Great War, he was working in the Riverina as an engineer on Canoon Station, Hay until 1930. He died on 7 May 1933.

Henry Bertrand

Henry Louis Bertrand was a respectable Jewish Sydney dentist in Victorian era. He ran a successful practice and residence at 7 Wynyard Square and seemed the picture of Victorian respectability, living with his timid but attractive wife Jane Palmer. Her parents opposed the union, thinking that Bertrand was 'a bad man'.

They and their two children appeared happy enough. Then Ellen Kinder had a toothache. It appears that Bertrand fell in love with her at first sight. By Ellen's second appointment the couple were showing each other physical affection.

Ellen was born in New Zealand. It was there she met her husband Henry Kinder with whom she had two children before moving across the Tasman. Ellen was not proper in the Victorian sense. She had at least one other lover, Frank Jackson. Meanwhile Henry Kinder was a well-liked head teller at the City Bank on the corner of King and George Streets. Kinder was given to alcoholism and was not in good health.

The Bertrands and the Kinders became friends and often socialised together. Meanwhile, the affair between the dentist and the banker's wife continued for about nine months.

Some four months into the affair, Ellen's other lover Jackson arrived in Sydney and Ellen and Frank continued their affair. The dentist was livid with jealousy. A *ménage á trois* was too much for him to bear. Jackson for his part seemed indifferent. There was a battle of wills that Bertrand won. In a strange twist Bertrand invited Jackson to move into his house at Wynyard Square. By this time Bertrand had already decided to get rid of both Mr Kinder and his own wife so that he could have Ellen for himself. He told Jackson, 'All things are possible, and time will show it. Kinder is rapidly killing himself with drink. If that won't do it, other things will.'

It's quite likely that he planned to use Jackson as part of his alibi. On two occasions he drugged the house guest and rifled through his papers, stealing love letters between Ellen and Jackson which he could plant on Kinder's corpse suggesting the motive of suicide — which he didn't use in the end. He then persuaded Jackson to leave town and then set about the second part of the plan.

Dressed as a woman, Bertrand bought a pistol. On 2 October 1865 arrangements were made for the families to dine together at the Kinder's house. After dinner Bertrand shot Kinder in the head.

Unfortunately, Kinder didn't die. Mrs Bertrand retrieved the bullet from her husband and she tended to the cuckold's wounds. The doctor was called. Bertrand claimed not to remember the circumstances of the accident and it was put down to a suicide attempt.

After all these mishaps, Bertrand made up a potion of belladonna and milk that Ellen gave to her husband and it finally killed him. The coroner found the death to be suicide.

With Kinder finally out of the way, Ellen Kinder moved into the Bertrand marital bed.

Things were not going well, however. Jackson attempted to extort money from Bertrand by going to the police. With full marks for boldness, Bertrand went to the police himself and had Jackson charged with blackmail.

This renewed interest in the case. No doubt Jackson also spilled the beans on what he knew. The police reopened the case and charged Bertrand with the murder of Kinder.

Things really started to come to a head when Bertrand's sister Harriet Kerr came to visit. She was shocked by Bertrand's brutal behaviour towards his wife Jane. He was starting to lose his mind too, claiming that he saw Kinder's ghost appearing in the house.

Fearing that Bertrand would kill his wife, Kerr went to the police. Once they started to investigate there were no shortage of witnesses to Bertrand's behaviour. Bertrand's sister testified that her brother had said of Ellen, 'Yes, I know she is a bad woman.' He said that was why he must marry her — because she was a wicked woman. He said he would make a second Lucretia of her. He then paused, and, leaning over me whispered, 'Kinder did not die by the shot, we poisoned him.' He said, 'She (pointing to his wife on the sofa) gave him the poison.' He said the poison would never be discovered, and that he had enough poison in the house to kill half the people in Sydney. He had also said it was very likely that before I went to Brisbane I should see his wife's funeral. According to Harriet Kerr, Bertrand had spoken about Kinder several times; about seeing his ghost, and when he saw the colour of liquors on the table, referred to it as blood. At one time he said he loved Mrs Kinder dearly, and at other times said she knew every wicked deed that could be committed, and that she was a devil's imp.

Bertrand's sister laid out the whole story to the police including details such as that Jane Bertrand had been forced to dress the pistol wounds to Kinder's head while the lovers walked around the room cuddling. In the weeks following the murder Bertrand tried to kill Jane and his sister.

Sydney was appropriately scandalised by the case — not least of it being the *ménage á trois* at Wynyard Square with Henry Kinder barely cold.

The police also discovered Bertrand's diary and a cache of very explicit love letters from Ellen Kinder to her lover the dentist.

His dentistry practice hit the skids too, so Bertrand bought an interest in the University Hotel in Glebe to save himself financially.

The case was one of the most significant affairs of the time. All the elements of melodrama were there in spades — lust, murder, poison, mesmerism. The role of Bertrand's wife was unclear. Charges against her and Ellen were not proceeded with. It was agreed that Jane was under the mesmeric power of her husband. The two women disappeared as soon as they could and were not heard from again,

Bertrand stood trial. The first jury was hung. The second found him guilty and he was sentenced to death. The Jewish community raised support for an appeal to the Privy Council who found that there were flaws in the second trial. Bertrand protested his innocence in court but then told many people including his counsel that he had done the crime. In the end he was sentenced to jail. He served 28 years — four of those in an asylum. He learned to play the organ and carving — one of his pieces is in the Mitchell Library — and was a model prisoner until his release.

Justice Stephen said it best when he pronounced sentence on Bertrand, 'You were madly in love with this woman, with a passion eating into your vitals; and you would have committed any crime

The Dangerous — Killers, Serial and Otherwise

to have her as your own ... You cannot but be regarded as a fiend. You are not a human being in feeling. I can speak of you with compassion, because I do not think you are fully possessed of the mind that God has been pleased to give to almost all of us. On that account alone I feel some sympathy.'

John Knatchbull

The eighth son of a baron Sir Edward Knatchbull, John was well educated and served under Lord Horatio Nelson as a Captain. He was born *c*1792, the third child of a womanising father. His early life was characterised by trouble. Although his rise through the ranks suggests some talent, he was often in trouble. He was eventually retired from the Royal Navy in 1818 but forfeited his pension due to debt. Hard up, Knatchbull turned to crime. In 1824 he was convicted, in the name of John Fitch, of stealing with force and arms, and sentenced to fourteen years transportation, arriving in New South Wales in April 1925 and was sent to Bathurst.

Knatchbull tried hard to adjust to convict life and was doing well. The colony was starved for aristocrats, so even one on the downward slide was the source of much interest in New South Wales. By 1826, he was a convict constable on the Western Road at Bathurst. He won his ticket-of-leave in 1829 for bringing in eight runaways under the Bushranging Act. But he couldn't go straight.

In 1931 he was convicted of forgery and sent to Norfolk Island in 1832.

On the way to the penal settlement, Knatchbull led an attempted mutiny by putting arsenic into the crew's tea. Unfortunately the conspiracy was discovered. Given that they were already on route to the worst place on earth, there seemed little point in a trial.

Knatchbull latter took part in the Norfolk Island Rebellion. He survived this too. It's not recorded whether he avoided the noose through his charm, his family name or just luck but he did survive. Unfortunately the war, the loss of his reputation and the disgrace to his family all preyed on his mind. He had fallen from the aristocracy to the lowliest of convicts. Then more than a decade of brutal punishment broke his senses. He was lucky not to have been hanged for his part in the Norfolk Island Mutiny. He was returned to Sydney to complete his sentence.

Then, in 1842 went to Ellen Jamieson's shop to see about a wedding dress and in a fury or a fit of madness killed Mrs Jamieson, stealing her money and a pocketbook which were later found on him.

His defence proposed that Knatchbull was insane at the time. It was the first time that a plea of 'moral insanity' had been tendered in a British court. In the event it was unsuccessful. He appealed on a technicality which also didn't succeed. He had cheated the gallows too many times. The case scandalised the community and given his background was the source of much gossip. In the event he was hanged on February 1844 in front of a crowd of some 10 000. Sir William Burton had noted, in reprimanding the court which had spared him on Norfolk Island, 'He can never do good.'

Jean Lee

In the first half of the twentieth century there was a definite distinction between good and bad women. Most Australians lived lives of quiet suburban respectability. There were not many lifestyle choices other than the straight and narrow. Occasionally there were women who turned their backs on suburbia and crossed into the fast lane.

Jean Lee was born in Dubbo in December 1919. Her father worked the railways and provided a plain but honest household for his wife and five children. The Lees moved to Sydney where was Jean was educated, briefly. She had left school by the time of her Intermediate Certificate. She may have been pregnant.

She worked in a variety of jobs from office work to labouring in a canned goods factory, waitressing, milliner and stenographer. By the age of nineteen she was married to Raymond Brees. He was sometimes a painter but mostly drunk and their marriage was violent even after the birth of her child, Jillian in 1939. They stuck out ten years of fighting and Brees' womanising. After separating from Brees, Jean found herself caught in the poverty trap of single motherhood and she gravitated towards petty crime and prostitution. Some accounts have portrayed her as a fundamentally immoral woman and others have sympathised with the problems for single mothers at the time.

In any event, she took to the life with some enthusiasm. He daughter was consigned permanently with her grandparents and Jean worked in Sydney and Melbourne, often under aliases. She became commonly known as Jean Lee.

Through her pimp, Morris Dias, she became further entrenched in the underworld. She met Robert Clayton who was a very violent criminal. He became her pimp and she was devoted to him. They were separated for three years while Clayton was in jail but the relationship resumed on his release. They were adept at running a con known as the Badger Game. This involved a woman picking up a man — preferably married and either a businessman or American serviceman. Once the mark (or victim) was back at the flat or car backseat or hotel room, a man claiming to be the woman's husband/ brother/ father would burst in and catch them at it. At this point the mark would pay money so that the police or the newspapers or his wife would not be informed. Failing the threat of exposure Clayton would bash and rob the hapless marks. Between May 1945 and July 1948, Jean Lee appeared twenty-three times at Sydney's Central Police Court, on charges of offensive behaviour.

In the spring of 1949 Clayton and Lee went to Melbourne for a holiday to celebrate his release from a short jail sentence. They also planned to work the Spring Carnival. In Melbourne Clayton teamed up with another violent criminal, Norman Andrews.

The three were drinking in the University Hotel in Lygon Street, Carlton and noticed Bill 'Pops' Kent. In those days, every pub had its own SP bookmaker who took small punts from the patrons. These small SPs were not a lucrative business and were seen more as a service to the drinkers than organised crime Clayton and his friends decided that King would be flush with his Saturday takings. King was an affable type and it was easy for Lee to strike up an acquaintance. The three friends were invited back to King's house.

Once inside there was little cash to be had. The gang tied King up and tortured him with lighted cigarettes and a severe beating to get him to reveal the whereabouts of his stash. In the end Clayton and Andrews strangled the old man.

The three eventually fled the house. However, one of King's neighbours had been watching the comings and goings and grew suspicious. She went to King's flat and found him dead. The neighbour was able to identify Lee by a sore on her nose — the result of a bashing by Clayton. The gang was arrested before dawn.

The public outcry was deafening. Although Lee claimed, and was supported by Clayton, that she had not hit King, but was merely an observer, she was given the death penalty. There was some call for her sentence to be commuted but the premier was resolute. At 8 a.m. on 19 February 1951 she was hanged — the last woman to be executed in Australia.

Eugenia Falleni

Even as an early teen, Eugenia Falleni wished to live as a man. Born in Florence around 1875, her parents moved to New Zealand when Eugenia was two years old. At sixteen she ran away to sea as a sailor and worked between Australian and New Zealand.

In 1898, she gave birth to a daughter Josephine whom she brought to Sydney and had boarded out. She then presented herself to the world as Harry Crawford and began working in labouring jobs and in private service. In 1912, Harry met a widow, Annie Birkett, who had a nine-year-old son, also called Harry. Falleni/Crawford claimed to be a 38-year-old widower, and he and Annie were married two years later. Josephine came to live with the Crawfords in Balmain. It appears that Josephine knew her parent's sex but Birkett didn't discover the truth until 1917. She did not take the news well.

Falleni/ Crawford took his wife on a picnic to Lane Cove River Park where he bashed her to death and burned her corpse. He picked up her son Harry and took him to Watson's Bay where he hoped to throw him over the edge. Unable to kill the boy, Falleni/Crawford appears to have reconciled to the idea of becoming a parent and despatched the child to live with an aunt. Josephine, suspecting the worst, sold the furniture and left. Falleni/Crawford claimed that his wife had 'run off'.

Two years later Falleni married Elizabeth King Allison. A year later a charred body in the Lane Cove River Park was identified as

Birkett and 'Crawford' was arrested. On his arrest on 5 July 1920 'Crawford' revealed his sex, requesting that he/she be put in the women's cells. The trial shocked Sydney. Falleni appeared at his committal in July as a man and then at trial in October as a woman. She was jailed in 1931 and took up the name Mrs Jean Ford, as she was required by the court to live thereafter as a woman.

Falleni never explained her motivation for her lifestyle. She died after being struck by a car in 1938.

Kevin Simmonds

Kevin Simmonds, who was one of Australia's most brutal thugs, came from a tough background. He was born on 22 August 1935 to parents John Simmonds and his young wife, Sheila Mary. Kevin was first admitted to a reform school at the age of fourteen for stealing and at eighteen he was sentenced to two years at Mount Penang Training School for stealing and breaking and entering. Simmonds specialised in safe cracking, robbery, armed robbery and breaking and entering.

Simmonds had never countenanced a career other than in crime. Consequently, he spent most of his life behind bars.

In February 1959 he was released from a three-year prison term only to be sentenced again in August to fifteen years in Long Bay Jail. At the end of that year Simmonds and his mate Leslie Newcombe escaped from Long Bay. They crawled through a ventilation duct in the prison chapel and on reaching the outside world hid for a night in shallow graves in Botany cemetery.

While on the run they broke into Emu Plains Prison Farm and when discovered by a prison guard, beat him to death with a baseball bat and took his gun.

The pair was pursued by the largest manhunt in the State's history that involved 500 policemen armed with guns, bulletproof vests and high-powered police cars.

Newcombe was captured in a couple of weeks. Simmonds stayed on the run for thirty-seven days. His ability to elude police made him something of a cult hero. Letters of support and a fan club sprung up. The public overlooked his ruthless and violent life, concentrating on the heroic story of a man on the run for his life. Simmonds proved especially popular with women, as he was renowned to be very charismatic and quite handsome

Simmonds was finally captured and tried for the murder of the warden at Emu Plains in March 1960. Such was the public support that the jury declined to convict him of murder but rather on the lesser charge of manslaughter.

Simmonds was sentenced to life imprisonment and sent to Grafton Jail. He was subjected to relentless brutality there — as he had been for most of his life. Reports say that his spirit was broken in Grafton and he was a shadow of his former self, shuffling around the prison yard with vacant eyes and the scars from cigarette burns. Reports of the treatment of Simmonds played an important part of the jail reforms in the 1970s. He hung himself in his cell on 4 November 1966.

Leonard 'Lennie' Lawson

There was little sympathy for Leonard Lawson, born in 1927. He was a prodigy as a teenager. While still in his teens, he created his character the Lone Avenger, who was a masked vigilante known for rescuing women in distress. These comics were a great success in the 1950s. Lawson was also a successful commercial artist and photographer.

On 7 May 1954 Lawson, then twenty-six, took five models to Terrey Hills for a magazine photo story. Once in the bush he produced a rifle and tied them up. He raped two girls and sexually assaulted the others at gunpoint.

Lawson was eventually captured after a massive manhunt. His execution was commuted to fourteen years. In jail he embraced Catholicism. He turned his hand to painting religious works. He was released after slightly more than seven years. Once outside, Lawson soon turned into a sexual predator. He was later to claim that he was quiet and subdued except in the company of women,

His next victim was Jane Bower whom he convinced to come to his flat to have her portrait painted. He tied the sixteen-year-old up, sexually assaulted and stabbed her to death.

The following day, Lawson arrived at SCEGGS at Moss Vale with an automatic rifle. He stormed into the chapel and took the penitents hostage. As the police attempted to rescue those inside, Lawson opened fire. He killed fifteen-year-old Wendy Luscombe.

Lennie was soon captured and jailed. The judge recommended that he never be released. Back in jail he returned to his religious art. In later years, Lawson's art took a decidedly more disturbing character. He began to make video montages from television images. *The Sun- Herald* reported that, 'Lawson's movies have clearly defined themes of sexual violence and aggression against women, sexual submission of women, voyeuristic sexual fantasies and sexual perversion, often associated with children'.

In 1972, he went berserk at a prison concert in Parramatta Jail. He jumped on stage and took Sharon Hamilton, a dancer, hostage. Although she escaped unharmed the trauma of the incident led to deep depression. She was hospitalised in Chelmsford Private Hospital where she fell victim to Dr Harry Bailey who abused her and stole most of her compensation money. She eventually committed suicide.

Lawson remained in jail. His petitions for release were unheeded and he died there at age seventy-six. He was Australia's longest-serving prisoner and served the longest continuous sentence — forty-one years.

Ronald Ryan

Australia's last man hanged became a cause célebrè in the mid-1960s. It was a case of a good cause for a bad man.

The Dangerous — Killers, Serial and Otherwise

Ronald Ryan was born in 1925 at Carlton, Melbourne into a battling family. His parents were alcoholics and they beat their only child viciously. By the age of eleven he was a ward of the state following the theft of a watch. It was the beginning of a life of crime. Although he eventually absconded from the home and went straight enough to get married, Ryan liked the life of crime.

By 1953 he was acquitted on a charge of arson. Three years later was placed on a good behaviour bond for passing forged cheques in 1956. A further three years on and Ryan led a gang of break and enter merchants. By 1959, Ryan was a notorious career criminal. In 1960 he was sent down for eight and a half years after pleading guilty to eight charges of breaking and stealing, and one of escaping from legal custody. Paroled after three years, he returned to robbing factories and stores. Despite his claims to be a master criminal, in late 1964 he was back in jail with another eight-year stretch.

On the night of 19 December 1965, Ryan and another inmate, Peter Walker staged an escape from Pentridge Prison. During the course of the escape, Ryan got his hands on a rifle and used it to kill prison warder George Hodson. The pair escaped the prison but their days were numbered. The number was seventeen. Killing law enforcement officers was guaranteed to bring the full force of the police department into the case.

On Christmas Day 1965, Ryan and Walker robbed a bank at Ormond and fled the state, having also shot Arthur James Henderson, an associate. They were captured in Sydney early in the New Year and returned to Melbourne. Walker was convicted of manslaughter; Ryan was found guilty of murder and was sentenced to death.

By the mid-1960s, the death penalty had become a political issue. Large sections of society from the Churches to the press to the political Left opposed the death penalty on humanitarian grounds. Ryan initially pleaded guilty and hoped that there was a reasonable doubt as to who had fired the fatal shot. Unfortunately the evidence against him was overwhelming and he finally confessed. Nonetheless, the anti-death penalty supporters ran the full course of appeals all the way to the Privy Council. Victorian Premier Henry Bolte, however, was determined that Ryan would hang. Appeals were exhausted and clemency was out of the question, Ryan went to the gallows on 3 February 1967 in Pentridge Prison. He was the last man to be hanged and had he shot only a civilian he would not have suffered this fate.

The Baby Farmers

In the nineteenth and early twentieth century, the plight of working mothers was appalling. Even working married women were often unable to live with their children, for single mothers it was even worse and unmarried mothers had an almost impossible task. Infant childcare was almost unknown and certainly hard to find. The demand for infant care created a completely unregulated industry of 'baby farms' where women would board children for affordable sums, paid in advance. No doubt there were many scrupulous child minders. However, the underhanded types found ways to minimise or avoid parental visits and maltreated the children often to the point of death. Sometimes the baby farmers would on-sell the children to childless couples. In other cases they simply killed the children. It was an easy living. Unwed mothers were often ashamed of having had the children in the first place and disinclined to go to the authorities. Baby farming was common throughout the Empire, including Australia.

One such minder was Alice Mitchell who was responsible for the deaths of as many as thirty-seven children over six years in Perth.

Mitchell charged 5/- per week plus doctor's fees. In an argument over payment of these extras, Mitchell brazenly called on the police to recover the debt for her. The cops in their enquires came to Mitchell's premises and were horrified by what they saw. They found the child had, 'Pus coming from its eyes, it was fly specked, extremely wasted and giving off an offensive odour'. It died shortly thereafter. The coroner found that the child had died from neglect. Unfortunately, a charge of murder couldn't be proven and Mitchell served five years hard labour.

Frances Knorr was perhaps the most vicious baby farmer of all. She was born Frances Lydia Alice Thwaites in 1868, the daughter of a tailor in Hoxton, Middlesex, and was known as Minnie. After a passionate affair she sailed for Sydney in 1887. She went into domestic service before becoming a waitress. She met German-born waiter Rudolph Knorr and they married. When not waiting tables, Knorr was a swindler and petty thief. The couple moved to Melbourne where their first daughter was born in 1892

Rudolph was caught thieving and sentenced to jail. While Rudolph was in jail, Frances took up with another seedy type, Edward Thompson. He proved to be the love of her life but the feeling was not mutual. After an unsuccessful attempt at a career in dressmaking in Adelaide, Frances returned to Melbourne and began child minding, mostly of illegitimate children. Rebuffed by Thompson she reunited with the now free Rudi.

Mostly Knorr tried to sell the children, but when that failed she killed them. She and her husband moved around Melbourne quite a bit, eventually leaving town for good and opened up in Sydney. However, a new tenant at one of their former houses in Brunswick in Melbourne discovered the body of a baby girl buried in the backyard.

The Knorrs were tracked to the Sydney suburb of Surry Hills and the police arrived as Frances was about to give birth to a second child. Meanwhile a second corpse was found in the Brunswick house garden. Knorr was taken back to Melbourne to stand trial. The case attracted a great deal of attention. In jail, Knorr had a change of heart, embracing the Bible. She was on one view an unfortunate young woman who had fallen in with a bad crowd and had faced difficult circumstances. She had genuinely cared for some of her charges. On another view, supported by letters to her former lover suggesting fabricating evidence, she was an evil, promiscuous woman. Her husband pleaded for clemency.

The Dangerous — Killers, Serial and Otherwise

After five days of evidence and argument, she was convicted of murder on 1 December 1893. At her sentencing, she said to her lover: 'God forgive you for your sins, Ted. God help my poor mother. God help my poor babies.' She was hanged at Pentridge Prison seven weeks later on 15 January, one of five women ever hanged in Victoria. Before going to the gallows she confessed to at least two more murders. She wrote to the premier of Victoria suggesting ways of regulating the childcare business. Her last words were, 'The Lord is with me, I do not fear what man can do unto me, for I have peace, perfect peace'.

Veronica Monty

Women serial killers usually stayed close to home. In the years between 1952 and 1964 there was a spate of poisonings, mostly by women, known as the Thallium Enthusiasms, using popular rat bait, Thallium Sulphate. This highly toxic but colourless, tasteless and odourless substance was taken off the restricted poisons list in the early 1950s to combat a rat plague. Because of its blandness, Thallium was easily added to food and beverages and six women were charged with administering thallium in the 1950s. It's likely that there were many more instances where the victims only suffered mild symptoms and so were never reported to the police.

One of the most high profile cases was that of Veronica Monty, wife of footballer Bobby Lulham who played for Balmain and

Australia. In 1952, Lulham conducted an affair on Sundays while Veronica was out at Mass. One Sunday, Veronica added thallium to a cup of tea, which her husband drank. It would have been fatal dose had not an anonymous tip off alerted the hospital. Veronica claimed that she had made the deadly potion for herself in a moment of remorse. She was acquitted but committed suicide three years later, in 1955.

The most enthusiastic Thallium customer was Caroline Grills. At age sixty-three, a great grandmother and standing all of 4' 5", Grills poisoned seven members of her family — four fatally with scones, tea, handmade chocolates and other snacks laced with rat poison.

She appeared to delight in poisoning her relatives. One son-in-law, who was almost blind from a previous poisoning, noticed Granny behaving suspiciously while preparing a cup of tea. He switched the tea and sent the original off for analysis. Then he called the cops. Thallium was found in her possession and in food and beverages that she had prepared. Two members of the family were exhumed and autopsies found traces of thallium. The others had been cremated.

It appears that Caroline stood to gain a financial benefit from some of her victims; some had been 'mercy killings' and the others she had killed for the fun of it. The Senior Crown Prosecutor Mick Rooney QC, said that she was 'a killer who poisoned for sport, for fun, for the kicks she got out of it, for the hell of it, for the thrill that she and she alone in the world knew the cause of the victims' suffering'. He added, '… the crime of murder is a terrible one, and when the killing is by means of an insidious poison, secretly administered within the family circle to an unsuspecting victim, which destroys him mentally and physically, while permitting him to linger on for months in wretched agony then the crime is a horrible one ...'

She was sentenced to life in Long Bay Jail. By all accounts she was well-liked in jail and was known affectionately as Aunt Thally. She died in 1960.

The Family

South Australia has a history of strange homicides. The most famous case of all was the mystery of the three Beaumont children who disappeared from a beach on a summer day in 1966. A nationwide hunt never uncovered any clues as to their fate. It was, however, one of those cases that struck deep into the nation's psyche.

In the early 1970s, Adelaide was gripped by the scandal of police targeting homosexual beats along the Torrens River and bashing 'poofters' for their own amusement. Perhaps coincidentally Bevan Spencer Von Einem was on the riverside gay beat in 1972 when a group of police had been poofter bashing. Von Einem saved one victim, Roger James, from drowning in the Torrens. The other man, Dr George Duncan, was a lecturer in the Faculty of Law at the University of Adelaide. He had only been in Adelaide for seven weeks. His death caused a national scandal and led to the decriminalisation of homosexuality in South Australia in 1975. It also led to change in policing in the other states with a more liberal approach taken towards homosexuality.

A concerted effort by politicians and senior police eventually put an end to the police gang targeting gay men. Although they escaped serious penalty, most of the police concerned were pensioned off or disciplined. Then, in the late 1970s another series of murders targeted homosexual men. These victims were tortured and killed, their bodies mutilated in a horrific parody of a surgical operation. The public and the police believed that the murders had been committed by a group of people whom they dubbed the Family. The police believed that the Family was a group of paedophiles that included high-ranking police and members of the judiciary, politicians and religious leaders. It was believed that they kept their victims for their pleasure and then killed them when they were finished with them.

They thought the Family was responsible for as many as 200 gay rapes in a ten-year period. Unfortunately there has been no hard evidence to support this theory.

In June 1979, Alan Barnes, seventeen, was discovered dead at the South Para Reservoir in Adelaide. Although, he had been missing for a week, the post-mortem revealed that he had died only the day before.

On 27 February 1982, Mark Langley, eighteen, disappeared while walking near the Torrens River. Less than a fortnight later, his mutilated corpse was discovered.

The Dangerous — Killers, Serial and Otherwise

Two months later the dismembered remains of Neil Muir, twenty-five, were found in garbage bags floating in the Port River at Port Adelaide. In June 1982, Peter Stogneff, fourteen, who had been missing for ten months, was found dismembered.

Richard Kelvin, fifteen, the son of a prominent Adelaide newsreader, was found dead in November 1983. Police believed that Kelvin had been held in a drugged state for five weeks until he was finally killed. Like the others, he had been subjected to surgical mutilation and then his corpse had been washed prior to disposal. The murder was consistent with the deaths of the other victims.

Although the theory of the Family was the most popular hypothesis, even among the police force, finally, investigations led police to Bevan Spencer Von Einem, an openly gay 37-year old bookkeeper. Von Einem was in the habit of picking up hitchhikers and giving them drugs. Substances that matched those in Kelvin's blood were found at Von Einem's house and his hair was found on Kelvin's body.

In the case of Alan Barnes, he had made the boy's acquaintance a number of times and on the last occasion had drugged him to sleep. Evidence was heard that Von Einem had told a friend that he was going to do some 'surgery' on Barnes.

Friends of Von Einem gave evidence that he had claimed to have been involved in at least one death. One witness came forward and recounted events on the night that Alan Barnes went missing. He said that Von Einem had been with a group of other friends who also appeared to know of his activities. Further evidence was heard that after Von Einem had drugged Barnes, he called another friend to meet him, suggesting a conspiracy of sex fiends.

The witness also said Von Einem claimed to have taken the three Beaumont children and performed 'surgery' on them and on two young girls who disappeared from a sporting event. Police believe he matched the description of a man seen at Glenelg beach at the time of the Beaumont children's disappearance. These allegations seem to be either malicious testimony or wishful thinking. Von Einem's killings were clearly related to his sexual preferences. He didn't need the high profile Beaumont case to make him one of the worse sexual predators in Australia's history.

Von Einem pleaded not guilty to the murders and refused to name any accomplices. Nonetheless, he was found guilty and sentenced to a 36-year-jail term — the longest sentence handed out by a South Australian court.

Von Einem was back in the headlines when a scandal erupted after reports that he was abusing new prisoners and being allowed to wear women's clothing. It's likely that he will remain behind bars for the full length of his sentence.

The Snowtown Murders

John Justin Bunting who perpetrated the most gruesome series of killings in the nation's history put Von Einem's reputation in the shade. The killings began in the outer suburbs of Adelaide in 1992 and continued until 1999 when eight bodies were discovered decomposing in vats of acid in the vault of a disused branch of the State Bank of South Australia in the village of Snowtown, 145 kilometres north of Adelaide. One policeman was quoted as saying, 'It was a scene from the worst nightmare you've ever had, and I don't think any of us was prepared for what we saw'. This grisly find led to the discovery of three other corpses.

The murders had been committed mostly in Adelaide and the bodies had been carted to various locations before finally coming to rest in the bank vault in early 1999. All of the murders had involved torture and in at least one case, cannibalism. They were perpetrated by a group of half a dozen misfits.

The leader of the group John Justin Bunting was born in a working class suburb of Brisbane in 1966 and worked for a time in an abattoir. Bunting was a teenage psychopath and would-be Nazi who hated paedophiles, drug users and homosexuals. He clearly enjoyed killing and exercised a charismatic power over his gang. His chief accomplice was Robert Joe Wagner

Bunting's first victim was Clinton Trezise. The young man was thought to be a friend of Barry Lane, one of Bunting's associates. He was lured to Bunting's house in the Adelaide suburb of Salisbury where Bunting whacked him over the head with a hammer and killed him.

It was three years until the next killing. The second victim was mentally handicapped Ray Davies, twenty-six, a friend of Bunting's girlfriend Suzanne Allen. It's thought that she accused Davies of being a paedophile. Davies was tortured before being killed and buried in the backyard of the house in Salisbury North. Michael Gardiner, an openly gay man and cross-dresser was suspected of being a paedophile and was strangled by Bunting and Wagner.

As the body counted mounted, so too did Bunting's blood lust. Perhaps out of sheer laziness or convenience, Bunting's attentions started to turn on his inner circle. Wagner had maintained an eight-year relationship with Barry Lane who went by the name of Vanessa when he was cross-dressing. Lane also had convictions for sex offences and was living on a disability pension. In October 1997, Bunting and Wagner tortured Lane by crushing his toes with pliers before they killed him, although they maintained his social security benefits. Lane's lover Thomas Trevilyan, who was found hanging from a tree in Adelaide later on, assisted Bunting in Lane's murder. It was initially thought that Trevilyan, a young paranoid schizophrenic, had committed suicide but Bunting was eventually convicted of his murder.

Gavin Porter was a former junkie and friend of Bunting's associate James Spyridon Vlassakis. Porter fell asleep in his car under the influence of drugs and was strangled by Bunting and Wagner. The next victim was Troy Youde — Vlassakis' half-brother and son of Elizabeth Harvey. Vlassakis accused him of sexual abuse and he was bashed with planks and jack handles by Bunting, Wagner and Vlassakis while sleeping. Youde was then dragged into a bathroom, handcuffed, gagged and had his toes squeezed by pliers. Wagner stood on Youde's chest until he was dead.

The Dangerous — Killers, Serial and Otherwise

Frederick Brooks was the son of Bunting's fiancée, Jodie Elliott, the sister of Elizabeth Haydon. Brooks was handcuffed, gagged, beaten, given electric shocks and burnt with cigarettes and a cigarette lighter. His toes were also squeezed with pliers.

Garry O'Dwyer was mentally handicapped after a car crash and living on an invalid pension. Bunting, Wagner and Vlassakis visited O'Dwyer's home and he was handcuffed, beaten, whipped with a belt and given electric shocks.

Elizabeth Haydon, a mother of six daughters and two sons from a number of different fathers, was the wife of gang member Mark Haydon. She was known to be 'slow'. Bunting and Wagner visited her at home while her husband was out and killed her. Her death aroused the suspicions that led to the unravelling of the whole case when her brother reported her missing. The fact that her husband had not reported the disappearance threw suspicion on him. The police bugged his house and that evidence was critical in the investigation. The barrels of bodies were stored for a while on Haydon's property and he later rented the bank vault in Snowtown.

David Johnson was the only victim to be killed in Snowtown. Vlassakis' stepbrother, Johnson was lured to the Snowtown bank on the pretence of buying a computer. There, he was handcuffed, beaten and eventually strangled with his own belt by Bunting. Some of his flesh was later cooked and eaten by two of the gang.

The remains of Suzanne Allen, a mentally handicapped pensioner and girlfriend of Bunting, were found buried in plastic bags buried above Ray Davies, the second victim, in the garden of the house at Salisbury North. The jury was unable to decide without doubt that she had been murdered.

Although this series of murders was undoubtedly a thrill killing on the part of Bunting and Wagner, they went to some lengths to continue to collect their victims' social security payments — amounting to some $95,000.

Bunting and Wagner's associates included Elizabeth Harvey, the mother of James Vlassakis. She died in 2001 before she could face trial. James Vlassakis was a heroin addict who was drawn into the killing spree and became a gruesome participant. He had been sexually abused at the age of fourteen and idolised Bunting as a hero and protector. Mark Haydon was the fourth member of the gang.

The trial of the Snowtown killers was the longest in the state's history and cost some $15 million. Vlassakis seemed to be the only one of the killers with any remorse and he agreed to testify against the others. Three jurors had to be excused from the trial as a consequence of their emotional stress.

The picture that emerged from Bunting's killings shocked the entire nation. This was a world inhabited by people who had been terribly damaged either by sexual abuse or mental handicap and they turned on each other with apparent ease. The killings had managed to go on for so long because so many of the victims lived on the margins of society and were not much missed.

Bunting was convicted of eleven murders and Wagner of seven. Haydon was convicted of assisting in a number of the killings and

Vlassakis was convicted of five murders. The South Australian government demolished Bunting's house.

Catherine and David Birnie

Some of the most horrific of serial killers have come from Perth. Catherine and David Birnie, were like a demonic Bonnie and Clyde whose reign of terror lasted only one terrifying month in the summer of 1986. A psychiatrist described Catherine as, 'The worst case of personality dependence I have seen in my career'.

The pair, both born in Perth in 1951, first met as children. Catherine's mother died when she was ten months old and she was sent to live in South Africa with her father for two years before she was returned to Perth to live with her grandparents. It was not a happy home and Catherine was not considered a cheerful child — she was socially inept and had few friends. Reputedly she witnessed her grandmother having a fatal seizure, leaving her further isolated. She was sent to live with an aunt and uncle.

Her next-door neighbour David Birnie was the eldest son of six children of violently alcoholic parents. They divorced when he was ten years old and neither parent wanted custody so Birnie became a ward of the state. Birnie had begun an apprenticeship as a jockey. He was dismissed for sexual harassment.

Catherine and David fell in love and became a teenage Bonnie and Clyde. Their crime spree came to a temporary halt in June

1969, when they were charged with breaking, entering and stealing goods worth nearly $3000. They also had in their possession a significant quantity of explosives. The following month they faced further charges and David was given two years and nine months jail time. Catherine was put on probation due in part to the fact that she was carrying a child.

A year later David escaped from prison and rejoined Catherine. They were soon apprehended and imprisoned. Catherine's child was taken into care.

On release, Catherine became a professional nanny. She eventually married the son of her employer, Donald McLaughlan, on her twenty-first birthday, and soon gave birth to the first of their six children. The last of the children, aged only seven months, was hit by a car in front of her and died. This incident may have triggered a breakdown.

More tough times followed, and in a few years she was living in a council flat, supporting her father-in-law, her husband and the children. Her life with McLaughlan may have been unpleasant but she appears to have coped, even under these difficult circumstances. It would appear from her history that Catherine was capable of leading a normal life without expressing violent or sadistic tendencies.

Fatefully, in 1984, she met up with David Birnie again and resumed their affair. She left her husband and children and moved in with Birnie. She was completely under David's spell and would do anything to please him.

After release from prison, David Birnie became a labourer—with a voracious sexual appetite. His younger brother James claimed that Birnie had sex up to six times a day, injecting tranquillisers and cocaine into his penis to prolong intercourse. On one occasion, lacking any better offers, he even raped James, his brother. In the meantime he collected pornography. James Birnie told authorities that at one point David had 'given' him Catherine for a night as a twenty-first birthday present.

David Birnie was working in a car yard on 6 October 1986 when he met 22-year-old student Mary Neilson. He suggested that she come by his house to purchase some tyres. When she arrived he drew a knife and took her prisoner. He made her a sex slave, binding her with rope before torturing and raping her. Catherine documented the outrage on film and participated with David in torturing the girl. The following day, the Birnies took Neilson to the local forest where she was finally killed and buried.

The couple now had a taste for this perverted sexual torture. They took to cruising the streets in search of prey. They picked up one victim hitchhiking. The next one was a neighbour whose car had broken down. She was given a lift by the Birnies and then, once in their car, was bound up and taken back to their house where she was raped and tortured for some days before being killed and buried in the forest.

In some cases the Birnies insisted that their victims write letters or called home to put police off their trail. They clearly enjoyed dragging out their torture sessions.

Catherine Birnie said she strangled one victim because; 'I wanted to see how strong I was within my inner self. I didn't feel a thing. It was like I expected. I was prepared to follow him to the end of the earth and do anything to see that his desires were satisfied. She was a female. Females hurt and destroy males.'

Catherine was indeed a keen participant, taking photographs of her husband and aiding him in the victims' torture.

On 10 November 1986, a half-naked sixteen-year-old girl wandered into the Willagee shopping centre outside Perth with an amazing story. She claimed that the day before, a couple had captured her at knifepoint and dragged her off the street. They took her to a house where the man and woman tortured and raped her.

The following morning the Birnies forced her to call her mother to tell her she was all right. The victim took note of the phone number (which later aided police in tracking and catching the Birnies). A knock on the door, she presumed for a cocaine dealer, distracted the Birnies long enough to allow the victim to escape through a window and slip away.

Detective Ferguson and Detective Sergeant Vince Katich who were investigating the other disappearances realised that they had a breakthrough. They arrested the Birnies the same day. Once in custody, it didn't take long for David Birnie to confess. 'Okay. There's four of them,' he said. He and Catherine then led the detective to their victims' gravesites.

The pair pleaded guilty to four murders and one abduction and rape. It was apparent during the couple's trials that Catherine was completely in the thrall of David Birnie and that she would do anything for him. However, there was no question of an insanity defence for either party.

In March 1987, they were each sentenced to twenty years in jail. When sentencing, David Justice Wallace said: 'The law is not strong enough to express the community's horror at this sadistic killer who tortured, raped and murdered four women. In my opinion, David John Birnie is such a danger to society that he should never be released from prison.' Catherine and David exchanged more than 2600 letters before David Birnie hanged himself in his cell in October 2005.

Eric Cooke

Perth's most notorious serial killer, Eric Cooke took retribution for his brutal childhood out on the citizens of Perth. Born in 1931 into a working class family, Cooke suffered with a harelip and cleft palate. Cooke's alcoholic father took particular exception to his son's deformities and not only refused to give him affection or encouragement, he beat him like a dog. He suffered severe head injuries from his father's hand and was, for a time, hospitalised in an asylum.

Cooke maintained a calm exterior — polite and shy and retiring — as he retreated into a very dark inner life.

By the age of eighteen, when he was jailed for theft, Cooke was an experienced thief and housebreaker. He also got a thrill from setting fires and prowling the streets late at night watching people having sex in their cars and houses. He was discharged from the army when his convictions came to light

He was model prisoner and, on release appeared to go straight with a job driving trucks. He married in 1953 and started a family that quickly grew to seven.

To all intents and purposes, Cooke was your average working stiff. However, he had returned to his old habits of voyeurism, theft and arson. He also took to running over pedestrians with his car. Suspicions changed however in 1955 when he was convicted of car theft.

He served only two years and, on release was soon back to his old tricks. On 29 January 1959, he broke into the flat of Pnena Berkman. She discovered him in the act and he stabbed her to death. Two months later Cooke, known to police as a Peeping Tom and a snowdropper (someone who steals women's underwear and masturbates into it), was arrested for loitering.

By this stage, Cooke had an entrenched pathology. His crime spree was not particularly related to theft for financial gain but as a general hatred of the world at large.

He began carrying a rifle to attack people and, on 27 January 1963, wounded a couple in a parked car in Cottesloe, for no particular reason. His blood was up. His next victim was an accountant, Brian Weir. Cooke shot him in the head.

Cooke's next victim was sleeping on a veranda and was also shot in the head. Cooke then knocked on the door of a house in a nearby street and when George Ormond Walmsley answered, he too was shot dead. This series of killings terrified the city of Perth. The randomness and cruelty of Cooke's spree saw doors that had never been locked before were now bolted. There was a huge demand for security dogs and firearms.

Cooke struck again three days later and the following month, killing two young women. Six months later Cooke killed another young woman in Dalkeith. He abandoned his gun in nearby bushes where it was discovered. The police staked out the site and apprehended Cooke when he returned to retrieve it. Cooke confessed to eight murders and fourteen attempted murders (including five hit and run attempts). Two of the murders had already been solved. One was the killing of Jillian Brewer, twenty-two, who had been bashed and stabbed in her flat on 19 December 1959. Darryl Raymond Beamish, a petty thief, deaf mute and child molester had been convicted of the crime, despite his plea of innocence. Beamish had been sentenced to hang but the sentence was commuted to life in prison.

The other was the murder of Rosemary Anderson, seventeen, on 10 February 1963 at Shenton Park. Cooke made the following statement, 'I, Eric Edgar Cooke, now of Fremantle Prison, say on 10 February 1963, between 9 p.m. and 10 p.m., I stole a Holden sedan car. I drove towards Shenton Park subways, near Nicholson Road. I drove the car straight at her. At the time I struck her, I was doing about forty miles per hour. I struck the girl with the right-hand part of the front of the Holden car. She was scooped up onto the hood for a couple of seconds and then thrown over the bonnet.'

Nonetheless, the police believed that her boyfriend John Button had run her over in a jealous rage. At the time of Cooke's confession Button was serving a ten-year sentence. Cooke later retracted his confessions for these two crimes. Then, shortly before his execution, he made a clear confession on these matters, even though he had nothing to gain by it.

Cooke was finally hanged on 26 October 1964, the last person hanged in Western Australia.

Cooke was a psychopath and a sociopath who, when not on a rampage, could be charming and likeable. When asked why he committed these heinous attacks he said, 'I just wanted to hurt somebody'.

John Button served his entire sentence for the murder of his girlfriend. It was only in the late 2001 that he was able to clear his name. This was in part because of the work of journalist Estelle Blackburn and her book *Broken Lives*. Cooke's crime spree was the background for Robert Drewe's novel *The Shark Net* and Tim Winton's novel *Cloudstreet*.

Dr Harry Bailey

Dr Harry Bailey. Australia's worst serial killer was like a character out of a cheap horror movie. Specialising in psychiatry, Bailey took an interest in a practice called 'deep sleep therapy' (DST). The procedure involved using large quantities of drugs to the make the patients comatose and then administer ECT — shock therapy. Developed by British psychiatrist Dr William Sargeant, deep sleep therapy had been used in Britain in the 1950s until it was discredited and discontinued in the early 1960s. Undaunted, Bailey and his colleagues ignored even Sargeant's safety procedures when they introduced deep sleep to Chelmsford Hospital at 2 The Crescent, Pennant Hills in Sydney's northern suburbs.

The treatment was used for all manner of ailments including depression, anorexia nervosa, stress, drug and alcohol problems, neuroses and schizophrenia.

Under Bailey's direction patients were given dangerous doses of drugs — to lethal levels. Bailey was determined to hold the record for maintaining the longest chemical coma. Shock treatment was administered whether patients had requested them or not and in some cases against the patients' express wishes. No account was taken of the patient's health or fitness. Records of treatment were not kept or if they were written down, written in pencil so that they could be adjusted. The nurses were often given free rein, with no training or supervision, on the administration of drugs

Antonios Xigis was the first victim of deep sleep therapy in early 1964. Five more victims followed that year. Thereafter, two or three more people died each year until the hospital was shut in the early 1980s. Other patients recovered from the DST but were brain damaged as a result of the barbiturates.

Complaints began to come to the attention of the health authorities and the relevant medical associations on a regular basis starting in 1972. However, nothing was done until 1980 when, media attention forced a government inquiry and finally a Royal Commission.

Among more than two dozen deaths were a 28-year old admitted for depression in 1964. Another was policeman Peter Clark, who suffered anxiety and was dead within five days of admission. One patient was admitted to Chelmsford for depression and while hospitalised developed pneumonia, kidney damage and haemorrhage from the bowel. One woman had been kept sedated, neglected and confined to bed for so long that her legs fused together.

One patient, Barry Hart, was admitted to Chelmsford in 1973 with depression. He left the hospital suffering from double pneumonia, deep vein thrombosis, pulmonary embolism and anoxic brain damage. Despite specifically informing the staff, in writing, that he did not want shock treatment he was administered it anyway. He told Channel Nine's *60 Minutes* that when he left the hospital. 'I couldn't feel my body. It was a horrible feeling. And all my head inside was exploding with white light as if it was blowing off its shoulders. And the oblivion. Next thing I remember I woke up and I had a tube up my nose and tremendous pain in my shoulders and I tried to alleviate the pain by moving my arms around. I couldn't do it because my arms were strapped. I went berserk. I yelled out, 'Get these things off' and I heard people running and noises and talking and then, nothing again. I had these tremendous pains in my chest. It was agony to breathe. It was like someone sticking a knife in and twisting it, and I complained about this and they said it will go away, it'll clear up. And it didn't, it got worse. I used to vomit and I used to bring up blood and one of the nurses said to me if I was you I'd get out of here.'

Easybeats singer Stevie Wright underwent DST to cure his drug and alcohol addiction. He left the hospital with severe brain damage and a greater drug dependence which has plagued his life ever since. Entertainer Toni Lamond had DST to cure an addiction to pethidine and has since had severe memory loss. More than twenty former Chelmsford patients have committed suicide following treatment.

Perhaps the most tragic case of all was that of Sharon Hamilton. She had been a professional dancer. While performing in a show at Parramatta jail she was attacked and taken hostage at knifepoint by a prisoner, Lennie Lawson. This triggered a breakdown and she was admitted to Chelmsford. Bailey had a history of interfering with patients. He began a relationship with the suicidal Hamilton. Bailey convinced her to giver him the bulk of the compensation she had been awarded for the Lawson attack. He forced her to abort his child. He treated her abusively and carried on affairs with other patients and staff. She eventually committed suicide. This appears to have triggered a breakdown in Bailey himself and he was admitted to Chelmsford in 1978.

The Royal Commissioner, Justice Slattery found, 'The deliberate development by Dr Bailey of Miss Hamilton's dependence on him was reprehensible' and his 'manipulation of her was deplorable ... [He] used this to dominate her and to influence her if only indirectly to give him money.'

The Royal Commission found that at least twenty-four people died under Bailey's care and at least 1200 more suffered injuries as a consequence of it. At least seventeen of the death certificates signed by Bailey were found to be fake. Although the death toll mounted, the other doctors, the state government and the professional associations did almost nothing to investigate Chelmsford and it was only the efforts of the Church of Scientology, the media, notably Channel Nine, that brought an end to Bailey. The Royal Commission found numerous cases of negligence against other doctors but no charges were laid. Bailey committed suicide in 1986 by drug overdose.

Ivan Milat

Two men murdered their way into the national mythology. They rode the highways in search of victims whom they brutalised, tortured and killed. Their exploits were so shocking that they became larger than life. The film, *Wolf Creek,* merges parts of each of these stories and attempts to make them a metaphor for the lethal Australian outback.

Ivan Milat was known as the Backpacker Killer after seven of his victims were discovered in shallow graves in and around the Belangalo

State Forest on the southern edge of greater Sydney. It's widely believed that Milat's killing spree was aided by accomplices and that it may have covered several decades. His brother Boris alleges that there may be as many as twenty-eight victims. The bodies that were found were foreign travellers whom he picked up hitchhiking.

Ivan Milat was born at Newcastle in 1941 to Croatian immigrant parents. The family of fourteen children and two parents lived on the outskirts of Sydney and eked out a subsistence living, often sharing one large room. Ivan's criminal career began early with housebreaking, car thefts, theft and armed robberies. He was convicted of the rape of two girls in 1971 but was later acquitted. At fifteen he was a labourer for the Department of Main Roads.

The family remained tight-knit and Ivan was well liked. However, from an early age he displayed tendencies that foreshadowed his later exploits. He collected guns and knives and frequently hunted in the Belangalo State Forest. He pursued violent fantasies and aliases. His brother Boris later described Ivan as a loner and immoral. Boris had some reason for his emnity as Ivan had an affair with Boris' wife that produced a daughter. Ivan also slept with his brother Wally's wife. There is evidence that Milat, although promiscuous, was also insecure about his sexuality and frequently had sex with men. There is some suggestion that the Belangalo killings were triggered by Milat being abandoned by his wife Karen and then again by his brother's wife Marilyn in 1987. The killings and disappearances raised suspicions with the police, even in the Milat family, but no hard evidence came up and family solidarity prevailed.

In 1992, he bodies of British tourists Joanne Walters and Caroline Clarke were found in a shallow grave in Belangalo State Forest. In October 1993, the bodies of nineteen-year-old James Gibson and Deborah Everist who had both gone missing in 1989 were discovered nearby. A month later, twenty-year-old Simone Schmidl, who had vanished in January 1991, was found. Three days later the search uncovered the skeletons of Gabor Kurt Neugebauer and his girlfriend, Anja Susanne Habschied who had disappeared in 1989. Another corpse, Diane Pennacchio turned up in bushland and the crime scene matched these other victims

All of the victims had been stabbed and in some cases shot. There was evidence of sexual abuse and rape along with torture. Fear gripped travellers out of Sydney and the Backpacker Murders became one of the major issues of the day. However, the police seemed lost for clues. The case gathered interest overseas. In 1994, an Englishman Paul Onions went to police with a story of how he had been hitchhiking outside Sydney in 1990 and the driver had pulled a gun on him. Onions had escaped, just. He was put in touch with NSW police and identified Milat.

In May 1994, police raided four houses associated with the Milat family and arrested Ivan and Walter. As expected they found weapons and trophies that could be traced back to the murders. Although police and the courts believe that Milat did not act alone, charges have not been laid against anyone else. Milat continues to protest his innocence.

Bradley John Murdoch

Milat's fame was eclipsed by Bradley John Murdoch, who is not technically a serial killer. Murdoch was born in 1958. He had lived most of his life on the fringes of society. He lived in Broome and in South Australia and regularly commuted between the two areas, it was alleged, often carting amphetamine. Murdoch came to the attention of police in 2002 after he was arrested for a horrific rape and assault. He had also been convicted in 1995 of recklessly using a firearm when he opened fire on a crowd at a sporting event.

On 14 July 2001, two young English travellers, Peter Falconio and Joanne Lees were driving along the Stuart Highway near Barrow Creek when their vehicle was waved down by a man, apparently with car trouble. Falconio pulled over and left his car to assist the man. His girlfriend Lees heard a gun shot. Murdoch then came and took Lees hostage, tying her up and putting her in his truck. Lees managed to escape and hide in the bushes at the side of the highway until she was eventually rescued. Falconio's body has never been found.

Lees' plight and Murdoch's trial gathered the world's attention. In December 2005, Murdoch, who maintained his innocence, was convicted by the Supreme Court in Darwin. Murdoch appealed the case, arguing principally that Lees had been influenced by seeing his photo in the newspaper. The appeal was dismissed in January 2007 and an appeal to the High Court was not successful.

Paul Denyer/The Frankston Killer

In the winter of 1993 the Melbourne suburb of Frankston was gripped in fear. A sadistic serial murderer stalked the streets and parks of the mostly affluent community. The killer chose his victims at random and there was no inkling as to when he would strike next.

The first victim, Elizabeth Stephen was murdered on 11 June 1993. Her throat had been cut and her body had been slashed in what looked like a ritualistic pattern.

Almost a month later on 8 July, Rosa Toth, forty-one, was attacked by a man armed with a gun. She was pulled off a walking path into bushes where the attacker tried to strangle her. Ms Toth put up a brave, fierce struggle. She bit her assailant's finger right to the bone and escaped to the road where a passing motorist rescued her.

Later that same evening, the killer struck again. His victim, Debbie Fream, twenty-two, had given birth to a son only twelve days earlier. She had gone to the local shop in Frankston for milk and was attacked. She was stabbed two dozen times and her body abandoned in a nearby paddock where it was found four days later.

Three weeks later he struck again on 30 July.

Natalie Russell, seventeen, was riding her bike when she was assaulted and stabbed to death — again with no sexual overtones. There was a strong lead with a yellow Toyota Corona sighted near where Natalie Russell was attacked and a policeman had taken down its details. The car was tracked to a local man, Paul Denyer.

Denyer was living with his girlfriend Sharon Johnson, whom he met in 1992 while working at Safeway's Supermarket. He had lost his job there after assaulting a customer. He applied for the police force but was rejected on the basis of his excess weight.

The police came to Denyer and Johnson's flat under the pretence of making routine enquires relating to the registration of the Corona. The police immediately noticed that the cuts on Denyer's hands. They suggested that he had been involved in a violent struggle and that their position on his arms led the police to suspect that he had been involved in one of the recent Frankston cases.

Paul Charles Denyer, twenty-one, stood over 6 foot with a frame to match. He was known to friends and acquaintances as John Candy after the portly American actor. The third of six children, Denyer was raised in Campbelltown, Sydney, until the family moved to Melbourne when he was nine years old. The children were not happy with the move and some had a lot of trouble adjusting to the new environment. Denyer was naturally a loner and with the onset of puberty he put on excessive weight, which compounded his problems socialising. He became increasingly interested in morbid activities such as dissecting teddy bears, watching horror films and avoiding the company of others. At the age of ten, Denyer tortured the family cat and hung its body from a tree. He had also, it turned out, broken into a friend's flat and tortured her cat and its litter of kittens before killing them and smearing their blood and entrails all around the walls.

His anti-social behaviour continued with car theft and petty offences.

Police asked about the murders to which he denied any involvement. He was taken to Frankston police station where he eventually realised that DNA evidence would convict him. He blurted out, 'Okay, I killed all three of them.'

When questioned by police, the man who was dubbed the Frankston Murderer showed no remorse whatever. He said he just wanted to kill someone. He simply enjoyed it.

'Just wanted ... just wanted to kill,' he said, 'Just wanted to take a life because I felt my life had been taken many times.'

Denyer told police that he was angry at how his life had turned out, He alleged that his brother had sexually abused him and that he resented moving to Melbourne and being unemployed. He also said that he had thought about stalking and killing women for many years and it was only a matter of time before he did it.

He told police, 'I've always wanted to kill, waiting for the right time, waiting for that silent alarm to trigger me off'.

The only person he did like was his girlfriend who he described, unfairly, as a kindred spirit. She was completely unaware of her boyfriend's secret life and showed none of his sociopathic tendencies.

At his trial in December 1993, Denyer received the maximum sentence, thirty years, for three murders and an assault and abduction. Denyer was not far from controversy even in jail. He took to calling himself 'Paula' and wearing women's prison outfits. In 2004, Denyer requested being allowed cosmetics — a request that was denied. He also began agitating to be allowed a sex change. In the light of his vicious crimes, any publicity Denyer received simply led to immediate calls for more a harsh sentences. The public sympathy for him was nil and the likelihood of a sex change no better.

William Blackstone

William Blackstone, a blacksmith and thief, arrived in Botany Bay with a reputation as a safebreaker. He tried his hand at various small crimes before he was drafted into a plan to stage Australia's first bank robbery, hitting the Bank of Australia that had established its offices in George Street, Sydney in early 1828. James Dingle proposed that he, Blackstone and fellow transported thieves Thomas Turner and George Farrell tunnel through a drain under the vault and break into the vault.

It took three consecutive weekends around Easter of that year to tunnel underneath the floor of the bank and into its vault but they were finally successful and made off with £14,500. Disposing of the money proved difficult and the accomplice who laundered the cash took half as commission. Not enough to retire on, Blackstone was soon captured on other burglary charges at which point he, facing fourteen years on Norfolk Island, sold out his comrades. In exchange for his treachery he received his freedom and passage home to England. The others were given the death penalty,

Blackstone was not very bright and before his repatriation he was again found guilty of stealing £20 and sent to Norfolk Island anyway. The Bank of Australia suffered an irreparable loss of confidence and went out of business in 1843. Blackstone returned from Norfolk Island shortly after and was murdered, presumably by one of his accomplices.

Crimes of Passion

The mating rituals in colonial Australia were a potential minefield. On the one hand there was a critical shortage of women. On the other there was the desire to create a civilised society at the end of the world, to maintain the standards of the home country.

As in Britain, in the colonies romance was a function of social status. It was a woman's task to marry and to marry well. This was a tough market and not one for the faint hearted.

Robert Hick romanced Louisa Rule for some nine months during the years 1834–1836. Miss Rule was the daughter of a Sydney surgeon who was by no means wealthy. Hick was a clerk. He thought the match a good one and asked for Louisa's hand in marriage. Plans were laid. Wedding dresses and furniture and linen were purchased, as was a wedding ring. Then, shortly before the ceremony, Hick received word from England that his uncle had died and left him £1000. His position in society had just jumped and Miss Rule was no longer good enough.

The Rules sued for breach of promise. The plaintiff's counsel, 'hoped to prove that defendant whilst a poor merchant's clerk would have been very happy to have had made the plaintiff the partner of a poverty obscurity, but when he got his fortune his mind had changed — he would not presume what defence would be set up; it only could be an attempt to mislead the judgment of the Assessors. After defendant had had daily opportunities of ascertaining the character, habits, manner, and disposition of the young lady, he had thought proper cruelly to abandon her. But he felt satisfied the verdict that day would convince plaintiff and others that they could not blast the respects of young women with impunity, and that even in New South Wales, honour and honesty was the best policy.'

The court heard that Hick didn't like his future parents-in-law and thought they meddled too much. There was also some suggestion raised that Louisa was not as pure as might be and that she had frequented hotels and the theatre. The court heard that the neighbourhood thought the Rule family to be of loose character.

The case was eventually settled in favour of Miss Rule with damages set at £10.

The following year the Rules were back in court. This time Louisa alleged that Mark Hillas had raped her.

Hillas had been a serious suitor to Louisa and marriage was talked about but Hillas had cooled on the idea. Nonetheless they remained friends. Indeed neighbours testified that Hillas and Louisa had been alone in her room for at least three hours. Other witnesses had seen Louisa frequently at Hillas' abode in Parramatta.

On the night in question Hillas gave Louisa a lift from her home in Windsor to Parramatta. Louisa alleged that on the way Hillas had driven his gig into the bush and ravished her. They had then resumed the journey to Parramatta where Hillas had taken her to his flat and held her against her will and once again had his way.

Hillas didn't deny that he had made love with Miss Rules but insisted that it was entirely consensual. Hillas suggested that the charges were brought in order to force him to marry Louisa.

Unfortunately for the Rules, the judge pointed out that despite ample opportunities, Louisa had made no effort to escape or display any distress. Witnesses testified to Elizabeth's happy and relaxed demeanour on the Parramatta trip.

Given the severity of the accusations — rape was a capital offence — the judge had the Rule family charged with perjury and marched from the courtroom to the jail.

Mount Rennie Outrage

It came to be known as the Mount Rennie Outrage and everyone associated with the matter came out with his or her reputations besmirched.

On 16 September 1886, Mary Jane Hicks was walking to an appointment in Castlereagh Street. On the corner of Goulburn and Sussex Streets she accepted a lift from hansom cab driver Charles

The Dangerous — Killers, Serial and Otherwise

Sweetman. The cab continued past her destination to the edge of Moore Park and Miss Hicks seemed not to mind.

At a quiet spot near the park, Sweetman pulled the cab over and hopped in the back where he made advances on Miss Hicks. She resisted a little. Suddenly, four young men arrived at the window and startled Sweetman. They bashed on the cab and made it clear that they wanted to make the girl's acquaintance. Hicks got out of the cab and Sweetman took off.

Mary Jane now in the company of the four youths went off with them. When they started to manhandle her she began screaming and she was rescued, this time by a local worker Bill Stanley. Soon ten or more members of what was known as the Waterloo Push surrounded him. Stanley was outnumbered and Mary Jane abducted.

By the time she was found at Mount Rennie, near Randwick, she had been raped by between eight and a dozen youths. She was almost out of her mind with shock and battery.

Sydney was completely appalled by what they dubbed the Mount Rennie Outrage. It would appear that a young girl, perhaps a little simple and a little flirtatious, had gotten herself into something way deeper than she bargained for.

The police swept through Waterloo and Redfern, rounding up members of the Waterloo Push. In all they arrested some fifteen young men. Some came forward and others were turned in. All of them had alibis.

Although Stanley and Sweetman could make some identification, Mary Jane was severely traumatised and her testimony was highly unreliable. Sweetman was also arrested for his indecent behaviour in the first instance, It was believed that he had abandoned a damsel in distress and that did not look good for him.

More than a dozen of the men from the Waterloo Push were committed for trial before Judge William Windeyer. The public wanted the blood of the perpetrators.

One of the accused, George Duffy admitted to having had sex with Mary Jane but says it was consensual. Another, Mick Donnellan, had a doctor give evidence that he was unable to perform the act.

The defence raised the possibility that Mary Jane was not the virginal beauty she was said to be. It was alleged that she had already had an affair with a married man, Matthew Doran and that her morals were not so pure as the prosecution alleged.

Judge Windeyer ran the case hard. There was a huge amount of testimony to get through — not least of which the extensive alibis of at least half of the accused.

The trial was gruelling, and towards the end of the hearing the court sat late into the night on a number of occasions. Often members of the jury were asleep, sometimes from exhaustion. As the hearing drew to a close Windeyer kept hearing evidence until two in the morning by which time he was the only one in the room awake. He then resumed the case the following morning at nine and addressed the jury for ten hours straight.

The jury considered their verdict for two-and-a-half hours.

When eleven participants were found guilty, Windeyer sentenced each of them to death.

At this point, public opinion began to swing the other way. It was clear that Windeyer did not run a fair trial. As hideous as the crime was, the public did not want to send innocent men to their deaths. There was a great deal of pressure on the government to overturn the sentences or at least grant mercy. The government finally adopted a compromise position and hanged four or the accused as a lesson to others and sentenced the rest to heavy jail sentences.

It was an ugly matter from beginning to end. Sydney has never been a city known for its morality. Things really slid after World War I. It was a time dominated by wild women.

Nellie Cameron

Nellie Cameron was the original femme fatale. She was born into a comfortable North Shore family in 1912 but the suburbs didn't suit her. In 1926, at the age of fifteen, Cameron caught a train to the city. She seduced the tram driver, who had a wife and kids, and was soon living with him in and around Woolloomooloo. Nellie Cameron took to the streets where her extraordinary good looks brought her instant success. Across William Street only blocks from Woolloomooloo was the suburb of Darlinghurst. The valley, bounded by Stanley, Oxford, Riley and Forbes Street, was a maze of tenement houses and back streets. At the top of the hill was Darlinghurst Jail. It overlooked a warren of iniquity. Many of the blocks in the suburb were given over to brothels. There were sly grog shops, slums and pubs like the Tradesman's Arms where the criminal element of Sydney gathered to socialise. Cocaine was the popular drug at the time. Where there's vice, there's violence. The working girls were accompanied by lurk merchants who lived off their earnings, provided protection and extorted money from anyone they could intimidate. As the thug's weapon of choice was the razor, the area became known as Razorhurst.

One of Nellie Cameron's early conquests was Norman Bruhn, a Melbourne criminal looking to gain a toehold in Sydney standing over SP bookmakers with his razor gang. Bruhn was not tough enough for the Harbour City. Nonetheless, he moved to Sydney and tried to establish himself and was shot in 1927, possibly by associates of Guido Caletti.

In any case, Cameron then came under the protection of Guido Caletti in 1927, who also ran a razor gang. Caletti was one of the toughest operators in Razorhurst running protection rackets. He was Cameron's lover and pimp for many years. Caletti's rival for Cameron was Frankie Green, allied to the famous madam and sly grog queen Tilly Devine. Caletti and Green frequently fought over possession of Cameron and her income. In a kind of diabolical *ménage à trois*, Cameron passed back and forth between Caletti and Green through the 1930s.

Cameron was clearly a woman of great attraction. The cocaine and the prostitution took their toll on her looks but she was clearly a woman to die for. Things came to a head when Cameron

The Dangerous — Killers, Serial and Otherwise

was with Green. A rival gangster Gregory Gaffney, an associate of Kate Leigh, pulled a gun on Green and shot him dead. Realising what he had done, Gaffney then organised a group of his comrades and went out to Tilly Devine's house in Maroubra to take the initiative in what would clearly be a gang war. He thought his only chance of survival would be to destroy Devine before she avenged the death of her henchman. Once there, Devine's husband Big Jim Reynolds shot Gaffney dead as he was climbing over the fence.

The following month a pitched battle was fought in Kings Cross between the razor gangs.

Cameron appeared to revel in the life of the underworld. She was fiercely loyal to her colleagues against the police and she never appeared much interested in progressing beyond the world of whoring and dealing a little cocaine. She seemed by most accounts, which were generally kept by her pimps, to have liked her career as a whore. She certainly didn't try to get out of it when opportunities arose.

Cameron was not afraid of a scrap herself. When another Sydney prostitute known as Black Aggie started to move in on her turf, Cameron challenged her to a fight. The bout, with both contestants stripped to the waist, took place in the back bar of a Darlinghurst Hotel. Cameron won decisively and then used her nails to scratch her victory across the breast of her opponent.

With her looks fading and many of her friends and lovers dead or in jail, Cameron took her own life, gassing herself in 1953.

Kate Leigh

Kathleen Mary Jospehine Leigh was born in 1881, the eighth child of Timothy Beahan and Charlotte Smith. The starting point for Kate Leigh's career in the underworld is a little murky. There is some suggestion that at the age of twelve she found herself at the Parramatta Girl's Home as a neglected child. It is clear that in 1896 at the age of sixteen she married a carpenter, Jack Leigh. From there she gradually drifted into the netherworld of Sydney crime, most likely through prostitution. Her relationship with Samuel 'Jewey' Freeman brought her into wider contact with the criminal underworld.

In June 1914, Samuel 'Jewey' Freeman pulled off two firsts at the Everleigh railway workshop. He and Ernest 'Shiner' Ryan did the first payroll robbery in Australia and were the first armed robbers to use an automobile as a getaway vehicle. Despite these innovations in larceny, the gang was thwarted and Kate Leigh, who was part of the gang, offered an alibi for Freeman. When he went down, so did she doing five years for perjury.

While Leigh was in jail, 5000 troops of the Australian Light Brigade went for a pub-crawl that started in Parramatta and ended in the city. This marauding drunken mob outraged the public. Consequently, hotel opening hours were reduced from 11 p.m. to 6 p.m.

So began the phenomenon of the 6 o'clock swill. For the next half century, Sydney pubs became bloodhouses. In the hour before closing time, drinkers would crowd the bar consuming as much beer

The Dangerous — Killers, Serial and Otherwise

as they could hold. Then the pubs would disgorge crowds of raging drunken men on to the footpath to find their way home for dinner.

Prohibition was not, as we all know, a success in the US and the de facto prohibition practiced in New South Wales had exactly the same effect. If people couldn't get alcohol legally, an illegal trade was bound to arise. In Australia, after hours booze was known as sly grog.

Beer was the core of culture in Australia. This was true of Australia than any other country. Beer drinking represented all that was Australian in the way that wine has done in France or vodka in Russia or rum in the Caribbean. Although the citizenry bowed to the wowsers and the Temperance Union, there was no heart in it.

The sly grog shop was, like the local SP bookie, part of the fabric of Australia. Even the NSW Attorney-General, Anthony Alan, was a partner in Phil Jeff's speakeasy 'Graham's' that advertised its wares in the pages of *The Truth*. The illegal trades of gambling and liquor were little different in Australia from the stereotype Chicago mob story that Hollywood has pedalled since the end of prohibition in the US. The effect, however, was to weave a criminal element into the fabric of society which inevitably corrupted public life. As in the US, many local criminals became folk heroes. The publicity and acclaim assisted the expansion of their businesses and often disguised a violent and ruthless streak that was responsible for many deaths and much misery.

Kate Leigh was one of the more prominent Sydneysiders for half a century. The press loved her larger than life persona and downplayed her ruthless streak. Her displays of community service belied an iron will and a willingness to have violence done to ensure her success as a purveyor of illegal booze.

Kate Leigh was a natural for the sly grog business. She set up shop at 212 Devonshire Street, Surry Hills, and was soon running more than one operation, becoming an organised crime entrepreneur supplying grog at extortionate prices, running after-hours drinking houses, prostitution, illegal betting and gambling and eventually cocaine.

Kate Leigh was generally regarded as, at worse, a necessary evil in Sydney but generally something of a benign figure. On the one hand she was a criminal running an extensive underworld operation. On the other hand she was a solid Irish-Australian woman thumbing her nose at authority and providing a service to the average working man; she was known for throwing lavish Christmas parties for the kids of Surry Hills and for looking after the down and outs she came across in her area.

Leigh, like her nemesis the madam Tilly Devine, was perpetually engaged in promoting her public image. She cultivated the press and in the 1930s was one of the wealthiest and best-known figures in Sydney. Her title 'Queen of the Underworld' saw her rule over a male network of gangsters who were loyal and protective. She continually ran foul of the law.

In 1933, having been convicted of dealing in stolen hosiery, Leigh, with police support asked the court to order her banishment from Sydney rather than a custodial term. The judge showed mercy and ordered her to Dubbo for five years and not to come within

200 miles of Sydney. Within a few weeks she was back in town and arrested. This time she went willingly to Long Bay jail announcing that it was preferable to living in Dubbo.

Leigh was, however, just as violent and ruthless as her rival Tilly Devine, especially after the Razor Wars of 1927. The violence ranged across inner-Sydney for many years. Rival gangster Snowy Prendergast made an attack on her home in 1930 and she shot him dead as she did the following year when threatened by Joseph McNamara. She was not charged with either murder.

After World War II, Leigh started to have some competition from serious rivals who wanted to get into the game. She was getting older and the young turks entering the market were even more violent and brutal than she. Her business, which had made her one of the wealthiest businesswomen in Sydney, slowed down considerably.

Eventually the authorities used the Al Capone method and sent the Taxation Department to do their dirty work. All her assets were seized for unpaid tax debts and she was declared bankrupt. She wound up penniless and unwell, living in a single bedroom in Devonshire Street until her death from a stroke in 1964. More than 700 people, from all walks of society, attended her funeral.

Tilly Devine

Matilda Mary Twiss was born the daughter of a bricklayer in Camberwell, London, at the turn of the twentieth century. By the age of sixteen she was already in trouble with the law, no doubt the vice squad. In On 12 August 1917, an Australian Digger, Sapper James Devine, in London with the 1st AIF made an honest woman of Tilly and married her. She was far from honest taking up prostitution as soon as he returned to Sydney in 1919. In 1920, Matilda Devine followed her husband and started a new life in Australia.

The Devines set up house in Maroubra in Sydney's southern suburbs. Tilly Devine went to work in Darlinghurst, around Palmer Street. She displayed an enviable entrepreneurial flair and soon graduated from the streets to running more than a dozen bordellos, becoming a notorious madam known as Sydney's 'Queen of the Night'. The 1908 Police Offences (Amendment) Act that outlawed men living on the earnings of a prostitute did not apply to women and through this loophole, Tilly Devine built up her empire.

Devine's business boomed in the 1920s. She ran a large stable of girls out of her brothels and on the street. When not on their backs, the girls were employed shoplifting from department stores such as Mark Foy's and David Jones. They were also used to roll drunks, deal cocaine and perform other petty crimes.

The area bounded by College Street, Oxford Street and Victoria Street, centred on the Tradesman's Arms on the corner of Liverpool and Palmer Streets was christened Razorhurst after the gangs of thugs who patrolled the area armed with cut-throat razors.

Big Jim Devine fitted into this milieu well, as did his wife. They were absolutely ruthless, merciless violent characters. Over the years, Tilly Devine and her nemesis Kate Leigh have become

The Dangerous — Killers, Serial and Otherwise

'colourful rogues' but they were among the most vicious characters one would have the misfortune to meet. Their clients were bashed, robbed and humiliated and their enemies came off even worse.

Devine had a system of recruiting new girls up the road at Crown Street Women's Hospital. Young girls who had fallen pregnant and despatched to the city for an abortion or to give up their child for adoption were easy prey.

Once enlisted these unfortunate women were encouraged to develop cocaine habits that further bound them into the 'life'.

The Devines lived a happy but rowdy existence at Maroubra for ten years. Things began to fall apart when Big Jim's eye wandered and also when rivalries with other criminals brought trouble to the Devine's door.

In July 1929, George Gaffney caused trouble outside the Devine's house after an altercation with Frankie Green over the attentions of one Nellie Cameron and Big Jim had shot him and an accomplice. A month later the rival gangs of Devine and Leigh fought a pitched battle on Kellett Street in Kings Cross using razors and pistols. Dozens of hoodlums were taken to hospital. This turf war had raged for some months and the riot in Kellett Street was the limit of the public's patience. The public wanted quiet on the streets and from that point the police enforced the peace. The corruption and vice remained but was thereafter contained.

Tilly left her husband, divorcing him on the grounds of cruelty in 1943 and moved to 191 Palmer Street, Darlinghurst, right at the centre of the prostitution trade. From here she continued to rule the neighbourhood. She married Eric Parsons in 1945.

She went into business with Phil 'the Jew' Jeffs in his notorious 60/50 Club and the upmarket 400 Club. Devine was always conscious of her public role and thought that money would transcend class and profession. For instance, in 1953 she sailed for London to celebrate the Coronation of Elizabeth. Through relationships with the press, both Devine and Leigh cultivated their public personae as charming, colourful characters engaged in a little harmless vice.

World War II brought a boom to the vice industry with American servicemen coming through town. As the Queen of Wooloomooloo, Devine was ideally placed to supply American servicemen with cocaine, booze and women at a reasonable price.

By the 1950s Devine was one of the most famous women in Sydney. Her birthday party at home in Maroubra was attended by a wide range of Sydney identities and was the talk of the town. She said, when asked by a journalist for a guest list, 'The names of the people don't matter. Just put in the paper that there were jockeys and barmaids, horse-owners, dog-men, tip-slingers, trainers, gay-girls, me bank manager, me interior decorator and some of me lawyers, Say this: say everyone was at Tilly's suburban menagerie except coppers, top-offs, phiz-gigs and other mugs.'

Devine continued to operate her Palmer Street brothel until 1968, However, in the 1950s and 1960s, Devine's influence began to wane as new operators came on the scene and took over her territory, plus a huge income tax and fines, slowly eroded her wealth. Tilly Devine died on 24 November 1970.

Thommos

Sydney's other vice during the 1920s and 1930s was gambling, ensuring that even today SP bookmaking is still with us. Until recently, the city also abounded in illegal casinos in every suburb. Thommo's two-up school, a series of 'floating games' started in 1910 by George Joseph Guest was an almost mythical place where real Australians gathered to watch the tossing of two coins. It was estimated that in the 1920s, Thommo's was making as much as £6000 per night. Although two-up was illegal, it was considered the digger's game and therefore the police turned a blind eye and did not crackdown on the game. Thommo's was the most famous game in Sydney and it became more established under Joe Taylor who took over the game in 1954 after Guest died and set up premises in Surry Hills.

Born on 24 November 1908 in Sydney, Joe Taylor grew up to become a boxer, a Rugby League player (later managing boxers and footballers), officially he described himself as a bookmaker and shipwright. Taylor was a 'magnificent, if unflamboyant, gambler at cards, horses or greyhounds and a well-known figure on the Sydney turf. He was a professional gambler who was known for handing out his winnings to the down-at-heel punters. In 1949 he relaunched Rose's Restaurant, 105 York Street, as the Celebrity Restaurant Club and it was soon the most chic establishment in Sydney with Taylor bringing American cabaret stars to Sydney, helping the club to flourish.

In 1954, the same year he took over Thommo's, Taylor opened the Carlisle Club in Kellett Street, Kings Cross, which became one of the most popular illegal casinos in Sydney. Joe Taylor, nicknamed 'The Boss', was the perfect host to the cream of Sydney society including the radio superstars, the judiciary and members of parliament. Women were not admitted and security was provided to winners on their way home. The police still tolerated the illegal casinos and perfunctory raids were often staged with plenty of warning to give anyone who might be embarrassed by a picture in the tabloids to get well away from the club.

Thommo's was successful and continued to thrive well into the 1970s. Taylor died in 1976 just missing out on seeing Sydney's gambling clubs transformed into fully fledged casinos.

The influence of the sly grog sellers and madams faded in the 1950s. The Vietnam War brought hundreds of American GIs to Sydney, and with them came hard drugs and serious vice. A new breed of criminal rose up to meet this new challenge.

Big Jim Anderson

Big Jim Anderson was known as the Iago of Kings Cross and was a prominent figure in the Sydney underworld in the 1960s and 1970s

James McCartney Anderson was born in 1930 in Glasgow, Scotland. He arrived in Australia in 1957 after working as a traffic cop in New Zealand and gravitated towards the nightclub business. In 1966, he was managing the Latin Quarter nightclub in Sydney.

'The Latin Quarter was a knockabout nightclub,' recalled legendary nightclub singer Norm Erskine. 'Some pretty heavy dudes used to get there, but nothing ever went wrong except one night when Ray O'Connor [a local hoodlum] got shot there. I was sitting about three tables away. I looked up, the next thing I know I heard this shot and I saw the bloke lying and the blood coming out of his head. It got a bit of a reputation after that, but after about three weeks it went back on the road and it was packed every night, couldn't move in the place and it was beautiful.'

In the late 1960s, Anderson formed a business association with Abe Saffron and during the 1970s managed several of Saffron's bars, nightclubs and strip-joints, including the infamous 'Les Girls'. One night in 1970, at the Venus Room in Kings Cross, Donny 'The Glove' Smith [a notorious standover man], hit Anderson, breaking his jaw with the lead lined leather glove that Smith used to wear. Big Jim quickly recovered and shot Smith three times. Anderson was charged with murder but the matter was dropped by the Askin government due to the influence of organised crime on all levels of the police and the state government.

In 1975, when Anderson came to wide public notice, he was managing the Carousel nightclub, the place where the anti-development campaigner Juanita Nielsen was last seen before she disappeared without a trace on 4 July of that year. Neilsen was causing headaches for property development in Kings Cross through her small newspaper. Anderson was not at the club when Neilsen arrived but it is generally accepted that he ordered her death.

Anderson was always considered a prime suspect in the conspiracy to murder Nielsen but nothing was ever proven against him. He was certainly involved in all forms of vice — drugs, prostitution, gambling and thuggery practised in Kings Cross throughout the 1970s.

Anderson fell out with Saffron in the early 1980s and became an informer for the National Crime Authority. His most serious attack on his former employer was to give evidence that the nightclubs kept two sets of books enabling Saffron to siphon off money, tax free, from his business operations. As a consequence of Anderson's actions the Tax Office pursued and convicted Saffron of tax fraud.

Anderson spelled out in detail the operations of Saffron's nightclubs and especially the supply routes for liquor between bottle shops and nightspots owned by Saffron. At the other end of the scale, Anderson also detailed the involvement of senior NSW police in protecting the illegal operations of after-hours clubs. According to David Hickie's book, *The Prince and the Premier*, Anderson was asked whether the poker machines in the clubs were legal he said, 'Nothing was legal at that stage.'

Anderson survived his feud with Saffron and died of cancer in the Blue Mountains at the age of seventy-three. The Juanita Neilsen murder remains one of New South Wales's unresolved mysteries.

Robert Trimbole

Sydney in the 1970s became an important part of the international crime networks. It was a murky world where CIA operatives mixed with drug dealers and money launderers, forming alliances with crime syndicates like the Mr Asia gang, which was run out of New Zealand.

Robert Trimbole was born on 19 March 1931 in Australia to Italian parents. His family lived in and around Griffith in New South Wales. In 1952, Trimbole married Joan Quested and the couple moved to his parents' house in Griffith before renting a house. He rented a garage and operated his own panel beating and spraypainting business. Business was not Trimbole's forte and with four children to support, he struggled to keep the wolf from the door. In 1968 he was bankrupt and his workshop mysteriously burned down.

After his bankruptcy, Trimbole travelled Australia repairing pinball machines and seemed to become very prosperous very quickly. In 1972, he opened up a restaurant called the Texan Tavern and a butcher shop in Griffith. He soon was able to discharge his bankruptcy and buy a large house. He invested in many businesses and owned a number of cars, speedboats and other conspicuous items. He sold his two businesses to an associate, Guieseppe Segi in 1973.

There were rumours that Trimbole's wealth came from growing marijuana in the fertile soil of the Riverina. His fortune was estimated at $2 million. Trimbole was indeed the conduit for the drug trade's marijuana crops that were fed into international drug syndicates. Like a Mafia don he controlled his region, including the corruption of local police and federal politicians. It's estimated that Trimbole's drug operations were turning over in excess of $3 million a year.

With large sums of cash coming through his accounts, Trimbole used simple schemes to launder the money. Obviously opening cash businesses like retail outlets and restaurants was one way of doing it. Another was the racetrack. He bet heavily and came out even. Trimbole liked the track and was heavily involved in race fixing. He was known as a large punter. It is likely that he used the races as a way to launder black money. He was quite successful however and it is likely that he had a number of jockeys on the payroll.

The local aspirant for the Liberal party, furniture storeowner Donald MacKay targeted Trimbole and notified the Federal Police of his activities in 1975. MacKay tipped off authorities to a crop worth $25 million in nearby Coleambally that resulted in a high profile bust and four men were convicted on Mackay's information. Unfortunately during the trial Donald Mackay's name was mentioned as the informant, giving Trimbole enough reason and purpose to take out a contract on MacKay. On 15 July 1977, Mackay disappeared from the Griff Hotel car park and has never been found. His locked van was covered with bloodstains, the car keys and three used .22 casings were found inside the van.

MacKay's widow and certain media outlets caused a furore

about the disappearance of MacKay and were relentless in pursuit of justice. Their efforts resulted in the Woodward Royal Commission that investigated Trimbole and his drug network.

Woodward found that 'the disposal of MacKay was the result of an organised plan He was disposed of by the organisation which I find existed in Griffith'.

Trimbole stepped up his operations, going into partnership with Terrence John Clark, head of the Mr Asia syndicate to distribute heroin. When two couriers, Douglas and Isobel Wilson turned Crown's evidence against the cartel, Trimbole ordered that they be shot. Which they were.

In 1981 the National Crime Authority tapped Trimbole's phone. Many recordings were made including some with heroin kingpin Dr Nick Paltos. The latter was heard to warn Trimbole that authorities were closing and Trimbole made pans to leave Australia. The phone taps came into the possession of journalists, including journalists at the *Age*. When their existence became known to the Costigan Royal Commission they were referred to as The Age Tapes. The material on these tapes and subsequent investigations lifted the lid on the Painters and Dockers — Australia's most prolific and successful crime organisation. This material led to uncovering the 'bottom of the harbour' tax schemes and a whole web of criminal activity.

Two days after the wiretaps Trimbole left Australia, eventually settling in Ireland. There he fought all attempts at extradition back to Australia.

Trimbole eventually left Ireland for Spain where he died of natural causes in May 1987.

Nugan Hand Bank

The work of Mr Asia and other drug lords was facilitated by organisations like the Nugan Hand Bank.

Frank Nugan was born in 1942 into the fruit and veg business; the family enterprise was based around the Riverina in New South Wales. Nugan became a lawyer and moved to the US to study in the 1960s. It was here that he first came in contact with the intelligence community. The Vietnam War was in full swing by this time and Nugan was known as a friend to the CIA.

In 1970, he started working with Michael Hand. The latter was a former US Green Beret and Special Forces operative in Southeast Asia. It's believed that he was very active in Laos during the Vietnam era training Hmong guerrillas under CIA aegis, a connection that led to close contact to the 'Golden Triangle' heroin trade.

Nugan and Hand went into business together in 1973 opening the Nugan Hand Bank office at 55 Macquarie Street, Sydney. While the actual business of the bank was never very clear, Hand and Nugan seemed to have had access to a broad spectrum of society; any legal, immigration or bureaucratic problems were always quickly sorted by officials high up in Canberra. At the other end of the spectrum they dealt with the Painters and Dockers in Melbourne and known drug lords like Murray Stewart Riley.

It was never clear exactly what the Nugan Hand Bank did most of the time.

The bank grew very quickly, opening offices in Germany, Malaysia, the Philippines, Saudi Arabia, Argentina, Thailand, Singapore, Taiwan and the United States. The bank also had an inordinate number of ex-military personnel on its Board and working as consultants, including retired Admiral Buddy Yates and one General Black. CIA chief William Colby was on the books as an adviser to Nugan Hand; his card was later found on Nugan's corpse.

The clientele was even more mysterious than the bank's activities. Known criminals Murray Riley and Kenny Derley were seen visiting the bank and the drug lord Mr Asia was known to use its services.

Australian police became suspicious when, in 1977, the Narcotics Bureau was told by a major heroin dealer, 'Frank Nugan and Mike Hand. They are bigger than anything you have ever seen here in the heroin game … if you caught these blokes all hell would break loose.' However, any enquiries into the Bank usually met a stonewall from ASIO or the CIA.

It is known that in 1975 the bank played a key role in trafficking arms to anti-communist forces in Angola and Rhodesia/Zimbabwe. There has been other evidence that the bank was involved in many other arms deals and money laundering.

By 1977, the bank's accounts showed assets of $1 billion although subsequent investigation revealed that the figures had been massively inflated by creative accounting and double counting.

The Nugan Hand Bank formed alliances not only with known criminals and American spooks but also developed contacts with ALP dominated councils in New South Wales. This began to unravel when questions began to arise with the NSW Corporate Affairs Commission, especially concerning the stacking of shareholder meetings with known criminals and standover men such as former NSW cop turned thug, Fred Krahe. Under public scrutiny, the Bank started to collapse.

By late 1979 the heat was really on.

In January 1980, Frank Nugan returned to Australia from Europe — he had met Hand in Switzerland. He bought a gun and two weeks later used it to blow his head off. Nugan's body was found in the front seat of his Mercedes just outside Lithgow on 27 January 1980. The police at the scene ruled the death a suicide and no forensics were done on the site. The case was so suspicious that the following year, Attorney-General Frank Walker exhumed Nugan's body for a definite identification, which was made courtesy of his curiously webbed feet.

Hand rushed back to Australia. A series of intense meetings were held, a dozen boxes of documents were taken off the premises and many more were shredded.

On 14 June, wearing a fake beard and carrying a false passport,

Michael Hand left Australia in the company of CIA operative and US Green Beret James Oswald Spencer. The Bank was under investigation and Hand was never heard of again.

The few documents left behind or subsequently uncovered by investigators showed that the Bank had losses of $24 million and had indeed been involved in arms deals. The CIA has refused to cooperate with any investigation into the Bank.

Squizzy Taylor

Joseph Leslie Theodore 'Squizzy' Taylor, also known as the Turk, was born at Brighton in 1888 and raised in Richmond. He was small of stature (5' 2") and somewhat shy — hence the name. Taylor was apprenticed as a jockey where he learned all he needed to know about fixing races. He was already involved in minor crime as a teenager being arrested at age eleven for thuggery and picking pockets.

In the years before World War I, Taylor ran with a gang known as the Bourke Street Rats. They were inner-city thugs who specialised in murder, assault, armed robbery, arson, blackmail, witness bashing, bribery, perjury, jury stacking, race fixing, gambling, prostitution, drugs and major theft.

The Bourke Street Rats used a popular method of extortion called the Badger Game or Gingering. A woman would lure a man into her bedroom and when he was in a compromising position, a male accomplice posing as husband or brother would burst in and demand money for his silence so as to keep the punter's name out of the papers or his wife's knowledge. Taylor played both sides of the game taking part in the extortion but also acting as a police informant to protect himself from prosecution. Between 1913 and 1916, Taylor was linked to several violent crimes including the Taylor the robbery and murder of Arthur Trotter, the robbery and murder of Thomas Berriman for £1,850, the murder of William Haines who refused to take part in a bank holdup and the death of Constable David McGrath.

Around 1915, Taylor formed a partnership with two-up king Henry Stokes and was soon the undisputed master of the Melbourne crime scene. His activities extended through gambling, robbery, vice and sly grog. Taylor set himself up as the mastermind of Melbourne crime and took a percentage of the spoils without having to get his hands dirty.

Taylor was rarely convicted after 1917 and became a key figure in an extremely violent underworld. His income came from armed robbery, prostitution, the sale of illegal liquor and drugs as well as race fixing and protection rackets. With an associate, Paddy Boardman, he ran an effective business of rigging juries — something that worked to Squizzy's advantage with his own criminal activity.

One of his schemes involved the abduction of young women. Kidnapped off the streets they were held prisoner and given heroin until they developed an addiction and were then more pliable to being turned out as prostitutes for Taylor's gang.

In 1918 Taylor arranged the robbery of Kilpatrick's jewellery store in which £2000 worth of diamonds were stolen. A faction in Taylor's gang was dissatisfied with the ringleader's cut and tried to overthrow the diminutive gangster. A protracted gang war was fought on the streets of Fitzroy in Melbourne's inner suburbs in 1919, known as the 'Fitzroy Vendetta', with Taylor being a principal figure in these gangland shootings

In 1921 Taylor was charged with breaking and entering. He absconded on his bail and a lengthy manhunt made no progress. While in hiding, Taylor frequently wrote to the newspapers, much in the style of Ned Kelly. He eventually surrendered in 1922 to police in a blaze of media attention. He was eventually acquitted of the charges.

While awaiting the jury's findings in 1922, Taylor visited the races but was warned off as undesirable. He returned that night and burned down the stand at Caulfield raceway, effectively cancelling the next day's race meeting.

In 1923 Taylor was involved in the murder of a bank manager during a thwarted robbery. One of his associates was hanged but Taylor escaped through using his political clout. Strangely enough Taylor and his second wife Ida Pender starred in a movie about Taylor's life, *Riding to Win*, which was banned by the Victorian censor.

Taylor faced charges in 1924 for killing a woman in a hit and run accident while he was drunk. He was acquitted. On the same day he was tried for harbouring a murderer and he received six months.

Taylor's greatest battle was with gunman Snowy Cutmore. In 1927, a feud exploded between them over the selling of cocaine. On 27 October 1927, Taylor went to confront Cutmore at 50 Barkly Street, Carlton. After a bloody gunfight, both men were dead.

Squizzy was a colourful figure on the Melbourne crime scene being a dapper man who strutted through the courts, racecourses and theatres. His constant written banter with the police that was published by the newspapers of the day ensured that Taylor became a larrikin legend, which is totally at odds with his vicious and brutal criminal activity.

Victor George Peirce/ The Walsh Street Killings

In 1984 the crime scene in Melbourne changed when a spate of police shootings occurred as a gang war raged through suburban and city streets, clashes between criminal clans and the Victorian police. These violent assassinations continued until 1995.

One of the flashpoints for gangland wars in Melbourne was the death of Victor George Peirce in 2002. Peirce was born on 11 November 1958, the son of Billy Peirce and Kathy Pettingill. His father died when he was ten and his mother became the matriarch of Melbourne's most notorious crime family.

Peirce was sent to reform school as a teenager. Once out, Peirce was involved with a group of notorious armed robbers, dubbed

The Dangerous — Killers, Serial and Otherwise

the Flemington Crew, and was implicated in a number of serious hold ups.

Pierce's friends and associates included armed robbers Mark Militano, Frank Valastro, Jedd Houghton, Jason Moran, Santo Mecuri. Russel 'Mad Dog' Cox and Gary Abdallah, most of whom were killed by police over a period of three years between 1987 and 1989. The deaths of these underworld figures triggered the spate of cop killings in retaliation and the violence in the streets of Melbourne increased.

On 11 October 1988, armed robber Graeme Jensen was shot dead by police. He was wanted for questioning in the matter of a robbery in Brunswick. Jensen had fled from the police and was shot dead in his car. The police alleged that Peirce and associates were devastated by death of Jensen and senior figures in the Melbourne underworld vowed to kill two police for every one of their own whom died.

The following day, two policemen, Damian Eyre and Steven Tynan. were lured by a call to an abandoned car left in Walsh Street. As they were examining the car they were ambushed and assassinated. It was later discovered that the shotgun used against policemen had also been used in a thwarted robbery at the State Bank in Oak Park seven months earlier. This robbery was one of many that had been committed by the notorious Flemington Crew, leading the police to believe that Victor Pierce, a close friend of Jensen, and his brother Trevor Pettingill were the prime suspects for the policemen's murders.

They day after Walsh Street, police raided Peirce's house. They arrested his wife but Peirce escaped over a back fence. The police demolished the house and dug up the backyard in their search for evidence.

Peirce's wife Wendy initially offered to turn state's evidence. She went into witness protection but later changed her story and was eventually jailed for perjury. Such was her commitment to her husband that she planned to have herself shot by Victor's brother, Dennis Allen, so that Victor could get compassionate leave from remand. The trial of the four men accused of the Walsh Street murders — Victor Peirce, Trevor Pettingill, Anthony Leigh Farrell and Peter David McEvoy began in March 1991.

Jason Ryan, a member of the Flemington Crew, became a prosecution witness in the trial and was offered immunity in exchange for his testimony. Ryan's evidence implicated many members of the Crew, including Gary Abdallah, Jedd Houghton, Anthony Farrell, Emmanuel Alexandris, but his evidence kept changing during the course of the shootings and then the trial. He was labelled an unreliable witness and Peirce was acquitted of the Walsh Street killings.

In the early 1990s, Pierce moved into the heroin trade with a vengeance. In April 1993 he scored an eight-year sentence for heroin dealing. He was released in June 1998.

On 1 May 2002 he was murdered in his car while parked in Bay Street, Port Melbourne.

The shooting of Pierce was a crucial step in the escalating Melbourne underworld wars in the first part of the twenty-first century.

Alphonse Gangitano

Alphonse Gangitano was born on 24 March 1957 and became an organised crime identity and the boss of the crime organisation known as the Carlton Crew. Gangitano drifted into criminal circles and found that he liked the life. He became associated with convicted criminals Graham Kinniburgh, Mick Gatto and Jason Moran in Melbourne along with the notorious Painters and Dockers. Gangitano became known as the 'Black Prince of Lygon Street' due his style of doing business, the snappy way he dressed and earning his living from extortion and illegal gambling and eventually heroin and cocaine.

Gangitano's most famous enemy was Chopper Read. The standover man turned author came up with a scheme to standover drug dealers such as Gangitano because they couldn't complain to the police. Read once arrived at Gangitano's house covered in gelignite, threatening to detonate it unless Gangitano paid $10,000. The enmity between them continued and Gangitano allegedly put a $30,000 contract out on Read. Gangitano left the country shortly before Read was released from prison in 1991.

Gangitano was implicated in a number of killings including; Giuseppe Arena, Jim Pinarkos, prostitute turned police informant Deborah Boundy and Australian Federal Police Commissioner Colin Winchester. Gangitano's activities also extended to armed robbery when he was implicated in the $2.3 million robbery of a delivery van in Richmond.

By the mid 1990s, Gangitano was one of the most powerful figures in the Melbourne underworld. His ambition, combined with his eagerness to wield violence, had given him a significant market share in the Victorian narcotics industry — both importation and its local manufacture.

On 6 February 1995, Gangitano and his chief lieutenant Jason Moran attended a large party in East St Kilda. An argument in the early hours of the morning developed and a convicted standover man, robber, thief and amphetamine dealer, Greg Workman, was shot eight times.

Gangitano was charged with the killing, on the strength of statements from two female witnesses who later retracted their statements and mysteriously vanished to Europe on permanent holidays. The police eventually had to drop the charges due to lack of evidence.

In December 1996, Gangitano led the Carlton Crew in an assault at the Sports Bar nightclub in King Street, Melbourne, allegedly extorting protection money. The gang viciously bashed innocent patrons — blinding a man and breaking a woman's jaw.

For the next two years Gangitano's power increased. Then, in January 1998, he was shot dead in his home. It is suggested that the Melbourne underworld had decided that Gangitano was out of control and that two of his closest friends, Jason Moran and Graham 'the Munster' Kinniburgh carried out the assassination.

Mark 'Chopper' Read

Mark Brandon Read, born on 17 November 1954, said he was given the name 'Chopper' after a cartoon character when he was still a child.

In the late 1970s, emerging from a troubled adolescence, Chopper gravitated towards the Melbourne underworld. In the company of like-minded friends he developed a skill for extorting money from drug dealers.

'My apprenticeship in crime began in the 1970s,' he wrote on his website. 'This had me robbing massage parlours and taking on contracts to maim and kill rivals. Once I had obtained a doctorate as a "standover man", robbing drug dealers and other criminals, who funnily enough couldn't report me to the police, became child's play. I once told a friend "why rob a straight guy of $20 when you can rob a drug dealer of $10,000 and he can't go running to the police?" After all, both involved some work on my behalf, but the man in the street was less likely to give up his $20 as he had to work hard for it. For the drug-dealers it came easy, so why would they put up a fight.'

'Read was a criminal sociopath with absolutely no conscience whatsoever,' said former Detective Sergeant, Armed Robbery Squad Rod Porter, who was Chopper's nemesis. 'He inflicted pain upon those that crossed his path. He was absolutely out of control.'

Read was convicted of assault charges and was sentenced to Pentridge Prison. He was to spend twenty-three years of his life behind bars. Once in jail he was determined to establish a reputation as a tough character not to be crossed, to reinforce this point he had his ears cut off.

Read was soon known for delivering extreme violence to others as well. He was alleged to have bashed more than fifty other inmates while in jail.

It was not all his way and he received a screwdriver to the chest. Then, in 1979, Greg 'Bluey' Brazel slit Read's stomach open during a prison brawl. Read attacked in retaliation and cut Brazel's stomach open. Read ripped out his own stitches the next day doing exercise. It's clear that he saw life as a jungle and that his survival meant being the toughest and hardest animal in that environment.

His most serious offence was shooting Sam 'Sammy the Turk' Ozerkam, outside Bojangles Nightclub in St Kilda, Melbourne, in 1987. Read pleaded self-defence and was convicted of a lesser charge. In 1991, Read also shot Sid Collins, president of the Black Uhlans motorcycle gang. He has denied the charge of malicious wounding.

Among his more colourful exploits were the attempted kidnap of a judge and the practice of strapping gelignite to his body and threatening to blow up himself and his extortion victim, unless he received a large cash payment.

In 1998, Read was paroled from Risdon Prison in Tasmania and married Mary-Ann Hodge with whom he had a child, Charlie. He later revealed to Hodge via the national media that he had married her as a means of assisting his parole hearings. The marriage lasted for a time but Read eventually returned to Melbourne where he married long-time sweetheart Margaret Cassar.

While in prison, Read wrote a number of letters to Melbourne crime writer John Sylvester. The letters were funny and gruesome, full of violence and dark humour. Sylvester and fellow journalist, Andrew Rule, assembled and edited the letters into the book *Chopper: From the Inside*, which became a bestseller. Read's stories were based on fact but full of bravado and embellishment. He claimed to have killed nineteen people and bashed scores more. His ocker, larrikin style softened Read's public image considerably. He was still a monster but somehow lovable.

Read continued to write stories that led, in 2000, to a feature film directed by Andrew Dominik and starring Eric Bana. In the public mind Read had gone from being a sociopathic thug to an amiable rogue. This change in public perception may have contributed to his early release from prison.

Fred Cook

Fred Cook, born on 16 November 1947, began his football career with Footscray in 1967, clocking up thirty-three games with the Bulldogs before switching to Port Melbourne.

Cook was named as Port Melbourne's full forward in its team of the century in 1970. He kicked a record 1238 goals in 258 games as well as winning a best and fairest and playing in six premiership teams in a golden era for Port Melbourne.

While still a player he had his first contact with organised crime. Cook claimed he was offered $1000 by SP bookies to throw a game. He claimed that SPs were part of the Aussie Rules landscape with up to $30,000 riding on a Port Melbourne game. After retiring from the paddock in 1984 he bought the Station Hotel, Port Melbourne. Best known as one of the pivotal venues in the Melbourne music scene in the 1970s and 1980s, under Cook's stewardship the pub went broke in 1988.

Cook developed a friendship with Dennis Allen. The latter was a music fan having shot Dingoes' guitarist Chris Stockley in the leg in an altercation in the early 1970s. Allen was a drug and gun dealer. Not only did Allen deal most of the speed in Melbourne, like Al Pacino's character in *Scarface*, he got high on his own supply, as did Cook, who developed a raging speed habit.

When not tending the bar or hanging out with Dennis Allen or boarding Jason Moran, Cook was a commentator on the Seven Network and one of the most popular sporting figures in Melbourne. In his other life he was very close to Dennis Allen.

Unfortunately the speed got to him. By May 1989 he had turned to crime to support his habit, he was busted for trafficking and scored a suspended twelve-month prison term and a four-year bond. His de facto Sally Ellen Desmond was placed on a bond on for trafficking in amphetamines and obtaining property by deception.

The following year both were back in the dock and this time Cook scored an eight-month stretch. Each time he was released he promised to go straight and within months he was back with Desmond on charges relating to speed, heroin and marijuana.

Cook has since cleaned up his act and remained sober for many years, having rebuilt his shattered life.

Dennis Allen

Perhaps the craziest of Melbourne's colourful crime figures was Dennis Allen. Dennis Allen was mad with rage his whole life. He was born in 1951 and grew up in a housing estate in Heidelberg, Victoria, and was the eldest son of Kathy Pettingill, a madam of a number of brothels in and around Richmond. Her children and their associates became one of the largest crime gangs in Melbourne, controlling much of the city's drug trade.

In October 1973, Dennis Allen was convicted of a rape that occurred during the course of a robbery staged by Allen and his brother Peter. It was his first conviction. That same year Allen shot musician Chris Stockley in the leg after being refused entry to a party in Melbourne. Allen served four years of his ten–year sentence for the rape. On leaving jail, he walked straight back into the Melbourne drug trade.

In 1979, heroin dealer and associate of the Painters and Dockers, Victor Allard, was murdered in Fitzroy, probably by Dennis Allen.

Police never had enough evidence to charge him over this killing although they did bring charges for gun possession and drink driving and he found himself back in prison.

In October 1981, he absconded while on day release. He was found paralytic drunk in the company of a prostitute in a Richmond hotel.

He returned to Melbourne from jail in July 1982 and took control of most of the local heroin trade by sheer aggression. He was the hardest in a town of hard men. Allen had a taste for amphetamines that fuelled mad rages. He. When on the boil, Allen thought nothing of shooting someone, even members of his own family.

The police kept Allen under surveillance. They busted a junkie Helen Wagnegg who was purchasing 1.5 kilograms of smack from Allen's house. Wagnegg later died in Allen's house of an overdose.

Police believe that Allen either murdered or was involved in the deaths of other underworld figures such as Victor Gouroff, Greg Pasche, Anton Kenny and Allan Stanhope. Allen was completely out of control, his violent rampages earned him the nickname Mr D — as in Mr Death. Among the many rumours that surround Allen, it is said that he ordered or committed the murders of several missing persons, including members of his family.

The kingpin of Melbourne drugs was addicted to amphetamine in a major way, which may explain some of his behaviour. He died of heart failure at the age of thirty-five as a consequence of his uncontrolled drug use.

Graham 'The Munster' Kinniburgh

Born in 1943, Kinniburgh began his career in the underworld with petty offences for fighting and the like. Kinniburgh was allegedly a safecracker for the Magnetic Drill Gang. This highly organised crew knocked over an American Express office in Melbourne for $350,000 and a jeweller for $250,000. Their greatest haul though was the Bank of New South Wales in Murwillumbah where a diamond-bit drill and astute panning netted $1.7 million. The Magnetic Drill Gang carried out more than a dozen heists in the 1970s and 1980s, including a $5 million haul of gold and jewels in Sydney in 1983.

Kinniburgh was allegedly involved with UK-based shoplifting group known as the Kangaroo Gang. Police believed that the Kangaroo Gang gave way to the Grandfather Mob. This latter group brought up to $1 billion worth of hashish into Australia in the early 1990s. Kinniburgh was charged over organising and fitting out the boat that was used to bring the drugs into the country but the Crown couldn't prove Kinniburgh's connection to the drugs and he was acquitted.

Kinniburgh was always close to the Moran family, the pre-eminent crime family on the Melbourne docks. Kinniburgh appears to have been involved in a number of major robberies, including doing over the house of trucking billionaire Lindsay Fox, and drug operations but always escaped serious criminal sentences.

Throughout more than three decades in drugs and robbery, Kinniburgh could be relied on to keep his cool. He lived well but modestly and never appeared in public looking like a mobster. According to Melbourne legend, Kinniburgh was capable of murdering those who got in his way and he was adept at manipulating situations in which he profited but left no fingerprints.

Kinniburgh seems to have been seen as an elder statesman in the Melbourne crime milieu. He was part of the old guard. His daughter Suzie married the son of a former Victorian Attorney General, Vernon Wilcox, QC. His son Brent became the professional at a prestigious Melbourne golf club.

Kinniburgh, known as the Munster because of his looks, was very close to Alphonse Gangitano, another organised crime figure. However, when Gangitano got out of control and started to bring police and political pressure down on the Melbourne underworld, Kinniburgh appears to have taken the necessary steps to keep the house in order. A judicial inquiry found that Kinniburgh and Jason Moran executed Gangitano at his home. However, there was not enough evidence to convict either of them.

On 13 December 2003, Kinniburgh was shot dead outside his house in the upmarket suburb of Kew while carrying groceries to his front door. This was a major hit in the Melbourne gangland wars. Andrew 'Benji' Veniamin was believed to have been implicated in this hit at the instruction of a Melbourne drug lord. In retaliation the leader of the Carlton Crew, Mick Gatto, shot hit man Benji Veniamin in self-defence allegedly in a dispute over the death of Kinniburgh whom Gatto referred to as 'Pa'.

In the volatile Melbourne underworld Kinniburgh was seen as a moderating influence.

Raymond 'Chuck' Bennett

The Painters and Dockers were Australia's most successful crime syndicate. One of their number committed the perfect crime at the Victorian Club in Queen Street Melbourne on 21 April 1976. The scene was the regular meeting of Melbourne's bookmakers to settle up the previous Easter weekend's takings. A gang of six armed men entered the room and collected between $1 million and $10 million in cash. Although the case was never solved, it's believed that it was the work of Chuck Bennett. He was affiliated with the notorious Painters and Dockers and was member of the Kangaroo Gang who carried out a series of daring jewellery robberies through Europe in the early 1970s.

Charges could never be proven against Bennett and the money was never recovered. However, Bennett was charged with other robberies in 1979. On the morning of 12 November 1979, while being escorted to court by two policemen, Bennett was shot dead. Two policemen, Paul Strang and Brian Murphy were rumoured to be involved in Bennett's murder.

Ben Hall

Born in 1837, Ben Hall was the son of convicts, making a living on the land at Wallis Plains near Maitland in New South Wales. In 1956, he married Bridget Hall, whose sisters were married to the notorious bushrangers, Frank Gardiner and John Maguire. Ben Hall and John Maguire jointly leased 'Sandy Creek' and established a stock of cattle. Hall had every intention of living a law-abiding life. It seems a turning point came in 1862 when Hall's wife left him for a policeman, taking their son. He lost the love of his life and easily turned to bushranging by his brother-in-law, Frank Gardiner.

In 1862, he was arrested for taking part alongside Gardiner in the $14,000 Eugowra gold escort robbery but was released on bail. During the weeks he was held in custody, his own property was attacked by members of the police force who were hellbent on revenge on Ben Hall for getting away with the robbery. His farm was burned to the ground and all his stock slaughtered. With nothing left to him, Hall threw his lot in with Frank Gardiner's gang, based in the Weddin Mountains.

Hall and his men held up mail coaches on the roads between Bathurst, Young and Yass. Hall's innovation in bushranging was to employ racehorses rather than the usual working horses. Hall maintained a strong discipline amongst his comrades in arms. Unlike many bushrangers, Hall's gang was not given to using force unless provoked. His daring exploits and his relative compassion in the execution of his duties made Hall one of Australia's most famous bushrangers.

In October 1863, the Hall gang made a daring raid on Bathurst. That same year they bailed up the entire town of Canowindra for three days. They took a police magistrate hostage and pillaged all the local stores, hotels and banks. Two police as well as members of Hall's gang were killed in gun battles and Hall himself was wounded. During this three-day riot, Hall's gang commandeered Robinson's Hotel in Canowindra and hosted a massive local party, at the end of which they paid the bill.

The following year they were operating south on the Sydney-Melbourne near Goulburn.

Following the shooting of two police constables by the gang, a bounty of £1000 was put on Hall's head. An informer eager for the reward tipped off the cops. With that information in hand, a party led by Sub-Inspector James Davidson found the Hall camp near Forbes. On 5 May 1865, police ambushed the camp and fired on Hall's men mercilessly. Hall was shot in the back as he ran away and his prone body was peppered with up to thirty shots by the police who ambushed the gang.

Harry 'Breaker' Morant

Born in 1864, the soldier poet, Edwin Henry Murrant arrived in Australia in 1883, a nineteen-year old in search of adventure. He changed his name to Harry Morant and gave himself the nickname 'the Breaker' after his skills at taming wild horses. He fancied himself a poet and some of his verse was published in *The Bulletin* magazine. Like many men of his time, Morant lived hard working on the land, drinking, womanising and taking his luck where he found it, even if it was slightly on the other side of the law, so be it. He married Daisy May O'Dwyer more famously known as Daisy Bates on 13 March 1884 and then skipped out on the bill.

Nothing appeals to an adventurer more than a war. Morant joined the South Australian Mounted Rifles and set sail for the Boer War on 26 January 1900. When the Australian troops arrived in South Africa they found the British bogged down by tradition. The British Army was designed to fight set battles against the professional soldiery of other nations. The Boer farmers were running a guerilla campaign with the competitive advantage of the support of the locals and an understanding of the terrain.

The commander of the British forces, Lord Kitchener, understood the problem and encouraged the creation of small mobile forces of his own. Australians like Morant were what the British needed. Morant and his best friend, Captain Frederick Percy Hunt, joined the Bushveldt Carbineers, a group that was encouraged by Kitchener to take the initiative and to act as brutally as they saw fit, especially to any of the enemy who disguised themselves in a British uniform. This was against the rules of law and the rules of engagement as they were then understood. Technically this meant that soldiers should kill the enemy on sight as once a prisoner is taken there are legal responsibilities that must be observed.

While on patrol on 5 August 1901, Hunt and group of Carbineers were ambushed by the Boers. Hunt was tortured, castrated, savagely beaten and stripped naked, eventually dying a horrible death.

On hearing of his friend's death, Morant, Peter Joseph Hancock and George Ramsdale Witton went in search of the culprits. When he found a man wearing Hunt's uniform he summarily shot him. He came on another group of locals and assumed rightly after an interrogation that they were enemy so he shot them too. One in the group was a missionary whom Morant decided, rightly, was a spy and he was executed.

Morant had made a fatal mistake interrogating these guerrillas as he had taken them prisoner. A complaint was made to the British Army that Morant had executed prisoners and Morantwas court-martialled on January 1902. Morant claimed that he had been acting on orders to shoot the enemy in the field rather than take them back to prison. Given that he was avenging the death of his best friend, and the brother of his new fiancée, he was proud of his achievement.

Lord Kitchener, for his part, denied that he had given the 'take no prisoners' order. It is now beyond doubt that Kitchener did in fact give the order. This was partly to protect his reputation as a civilised man.

The farcical nature of the court martial was further demonstrated when the courtroom came under fire and the accused left the dock, took up arms and helped repel a Boer attack.

Morant and Peter Joseph Hancock were sentenced to death on 4 February 1902 and were executed by firing squad on 27 February 1902. Morant's last words were, 'Shoot straight, you bastards. Don't make a mess of it'.

Henry Redford

Henry Arthur Redford, born in 1842, was a bushman and drover extraordinaire. Working in the far reaches of Western Queensland, Redford was struck by the vastness of the properties and herds, He thought that it was an opportunity for cattle duffing or stealing. He saw his opportunity on the massive Bowen Downs Station in western Queensland where 60,000 head of cattle were spread over 1,744,000 acres. Redford assumed that 1000 head would not be missed.

Having built his own cattle yards and accumulated his herd — including a prize white bull he brazenly drove the cattle down to South Australia. The region had not yet been explored, which he took to be an advantage in the plan. Redford was an excellent bushman and he believed that recent rains would have swelled the inland rivers and provided plenty of feed and water for the journey

In March 1870, Redford and his gang led the cattle down the Barcoo to Cooper's Creek and then Strzelecki Creek. In June, running short of supplies, he stopped near Hill Station and exchanged three of his herd, including the fateful white bull, for provisions.

Redford reached Blanchwater Station in South Australia and sold his herd for £5000. Apparrently home free, Redford was given up by one of his accomplices and an overseerer followed Redford's tracks with steadfast courage. He eventually came across the white bull and put the puzzle together. Redford was arrested in January 1872.

By the time the trial began in February 1873, Redford was a folk hero. His journey was the stuff of legend. His criminal odyssey had done as much as any man to open up the interior. The jury would not convict him and he walked away free.

Redford mostly concentrated on developing his own holdings — except for another small charge of cattle theft — and to droving. He undertook another heroic journey from the Atherton Tablelands south to Dubbo. Redford drowned in Corella Creek in March 1901.

Jimmy Governor

Jimmy Governor was known as the last of the bushrangers. His story as told in Thomas Keneally's novel, *The Chant of Jimmy Blacksmith*, (which was later made into a feature film by Fred Schepsi), is also a tragic story that illustrates the problems of black/white relations in the first two centuries of European occupation

Jimmy Governor was born in 1867, a three-quarter caste Aboriginal man stuck between two worlds. Governor was a handy cricketer and farm worker and a very adept tracker who sometimes worked for the police around Gulgong and Singleton in New South Wales. Baptised into the Church of England, he could read and write better than most of the white people he met.

Governor married a white girl, the sixteen-year-old Ethel Mary Jane Page, at Gulgong in 1900. They were apparently very much in love but mixed race marriages were frowned upon. His mother-in-law opposed the marriage.

Governor found work and accommodation for his wife and their child at Breelong. John Mawbey who employed him seems to have been more modern than most farmers, paying Aboriginals at the same rate as white workers. However, the domestic bliss was not to last. Some of Governor's extended family came to live with them and that appears to have been the breaking point. Governor was smarting under the prejudice of white society, combined with the pressure of supporting a young family, Jimmy became jealous that his brother Joe had designs on his wife.

On 20 July 1900, Ethel Governor was abused by Mrs Mawbrey when she went to the homestead in search of provisions. It was one insult too many. That night, Governor and his friend Jacky Underwood returned to the homestead and brutally beat Mrs Mawbrey, another woman in the house and three children to death. They realised that they had crossed a line and returned to the camp long enough to collect Jimmy's brother Joe and then go bush.

For two months Jimmy Governor and his gang terrorised the district. They attacked homesteads and killed women, children and a seventy-three-year-old man. A force of 200 police and 2000 vigilantes pursued the gang. The bounty on Jimmy's head eventually reached £1000. Underwood went off on his own and was captured. The Governor brothers were engaged in a gunfight shortly with Jimmy being wounded in the mouth. Unable to eat his strength faded. He was eventually caught on 27 October 1900 and taken to Sydney for trial. He was hanged in Darlinghurst Jail in January 1901.

Daniel 'Mad Dog' Morgan

Daniel Morgan was born in 1830 in Sydney and was raised in the Riverina by John Roberts. Trained as a bushman and stockman, Morgan was soon stealing horses. He was first charged for horse stealing at Campbelltown in 1847. He was arrested again in 1854 for theft. Six years later he was back in the Riverina, now a hardened criminal. He earned the sobriquet 'Mad Dog' after the sheer brutality of his crimes. The price on his head reached £1000.

Morgan's last stand was at Peechelba Station near Wangaratta in April 1865. He took the farmer hostage but one farmhand escaped and returned with a squad of police. Morgan was felled by a marksman and his corpse was taken to Wangaratta where it was decapitated and castrated. His scrotum was made into a tobacco pouch.

Many of the nineteenth century bushrangers became folk heroes but Morgan had none of their redeeming qualities — he was vicious and greedy. A memorable film, *Mad Dog Morgan*, was made of the legend by Philippe Mora and starring Dennis Hopper.

Mary Ann Bugg

The greatest woman bushranger, was motivated by love. Mary Ann Bugg was born to a convict shepherd named James Brigg and an Aboriginal woman, Charlotte, in 1834. Mary went on to domestic service and at the age of fourteen married a Mudgee shepherd Edmund Baker with whom she had a son. The couple were employed by a Mrs Garbutt, whose son James was involved with a former drover and station hand turned cattle thief named Frederick Ward. Around 1960 Mary Ann's husband died and she took up with Frederick Ward, also known as Captain Thunderbolt, one of the most famous bushrangers of the time.

When Ward was arrested and sentenced to prison on Cockatoo Island in Sydney Harbour, Mary was two weeks from the birth of their daughter. Mary secured a job as a domestic in the harbourside suburb of Balmain and at night she swam across the harbour to bring supplies to the imprisoned Ward. In 1863, he escaped from jail and the family returned north to the Culgoa River near Bourke with their two children. Ward worked through the Hunter Valley and as far north as the Queensland border. The bush skills Bugg learned from her mother were a great help to the couple's survival in the bush. Also being Aboriginal, Mary Ann could come and go in towns without being noticed. She often scouted banks and other targets had the potential to be raided by Ward. Her only risk was being arrested, as happened, on vagrancy charges. Ward for his part appears to have been an honourable enough bushranger and was not violent towards the innocent.

In 1866, the couple had another child. Mary Ann was devoted to Ward and was his constant companion. The hardships of the fugitive life took their toll and Mary Ann died of pneumonia at a squatter's home near Muswellbrook in 1867 at the age of twenty-eight.

Thrree years after Mary Ann's death, Ward was shot in an ambush. He was New South Wales's most successful bushranger and was idealised as a romantic figure of the time.

Ned Kelly

Ned Kelly has come to personify the Australian bush hero for his defiance of the colonial authorities. He was born in Victoria on 3 June 1855, the son of Irish immigrants. As a young man, Kelly clashed with police but was unfairly treated by the English overlords and rebelled, showing great courage and fortitude.

Caught stealing pigs, Ned's father John was sentenced to seven years of penal servitude in Van Dieman's Land and was transported in 1843. John Kelly died when Ned was eleven, leaving a wife, Ellen, and seven children on a selection at Greta in the northeast of

Victoria, now known as Kelly Country. Life for selectors — farmers with small holdings — was tough. There was little money around. The troopers imperiously harassed these tenant farmers and the Irish were considered less than respectable and the authorities believed they were justified in pursuing the Kellys.

The Kellys were well known in the district and it is likely that they lived on the edge of the law, and possibly some of the family's associates were cattle thieves. Ellen's second husband was a cattle thief and she sent Ned to work for him.

In 1869, young Kelly was arrested for assaulting a Chinese pig farmer who claimed he was robbed by Kelly but who Kelly said had argued with his sister Annie and Ned was only upholding his sister's honour. Kelly was arrested, spending ten days in custody. From this point on Kelly was regarded by police as a juvenile bushranger. At age fifteen Ned, in a moment of sardonic humour, sent a pair of calf testicles to a local matron and he wound up in jail for six months. Shortly after his release he was wrongly convicted of illegal horse-trading and was sentenced to three years. Again, shortly after his release he was charged with riding a horse on the footpath and again jailed. By this stage Kelly had no love for authority.

In April 1878, Constable Fitzpatrick went to the Kelly home with a warrant to arrest Dan Kelly on a charge of horse theft. While there he supposedly made a pass at Ellen Kelly's daughter, Kate. Ellen responded by hitting his hand with a coal shovel. Fitzpatrick decided to take revenge and claimed that revolvers were used and

The Dangerous — Killers, Serial and Otherwise

Ellen, along with a baby daughter Alice, was taken into custody. Fitzpatrick also claimed that Ned and Dan attacked him (despite Ned being out of the state).

Knowing how the authorities would react, Dan Kelly went bush and Ned, by virtue of Fitzpatrick's allegations, was branded an outlaw. The police arrested the rest of the family and Judge Redmond Barry sentenced Ellen Kelly to three years hard labour.

The Kelly brothers were joined by friends, Steve Hart and Joe Byrne, at their camp in the Wombat Ranges. The troopers, led by Sergeant Kennedy, set off to search for the Kelly Gang.

At Stringybark Creek on 25 October 1878, Ned came upon the camp made by Sergeant Kennedy, Constables Lonigan, Scanlon and McIntyre. The next morning the Kelly Gang ambushed McIntyre and Lonigan and the latter were shot in the gunfight. Scanlon and Kennedy returned from patrol and were also shot. McIntyre escaped and hid down a wombat hole.

After news of the ambush spread, a bounty of £2000 was placed on Kelly's head. The troopers increased pressure on the local farmers to give up the gang but this only increased the public's sympathy for them.

On 10 December 1878 the Kelly Gang took over Faithful Creek station near Euroa and took the inhabitants hostage. The following day the Kelly brothers and Steve Hart robbed the local bank.

Two months later, on 8 February 1879, they held up the Jerilderie Bank of New South Wales. No one was killed in either incident. It was here that Ned Kelly dictated his famous manifesto, the Jerilderie Letter, that described his view of his activities and the treatment of his family and the treatment of the Irish Catholics persecuted by the English and Irish Protestant squatters.

Kelly began to see himself as a revolutionary. There is evidence that he hoped to cause an uprising amongst the farmers and create a separate state in northern Victoria. As Kelly's ego expanded, so did his paranoia. A friend, Aaron Sherritt, was executed by Joe Byrne after the gang discovered he was a police informant. The Kelly Gang continued bushranging, holding up banks as far afield as southern New South Wales.

Kelly had seen pictures of the *Monitor*, an armoured battleship used in the American Civil War. He fashioned armoured suits adapted from the design of the ship. In a fatal design flaw, the massive weight of the suits, forged from stolen and donated plow parts, precluded body armour for the legs.

With another manifesto ready for delivery, Kelly came to the town of Glenrowan. He derailed the train outside the town to thwart the trainload of troopers he knew were on his tail. He bailed up the townsfolk, gathered them in the pub and had the bar turned on. During all the festivities, schoolteacher Thomas Curnow slipped away. He caught up with the train and explained Kelly's plan to the troopers.

Forewarned, the troopers set up a siege of the town and closed in. The Kelly Gang made its final stand at the Glenrowan Hotel on 28 June 1880. Although he could have escaped, Kelly returned to the hotel to fight alongside his comrades. By the time he was captured, Kelly had taken 28 gunshot wounds to his body.

Kelly was captured and taken to Melbourne for trial but far from being recognised as a criminal, he was hailed as a hero. Ned Kelly stood trial and was sentenced to death by Irish-born judge, Justice Raymond Barry. Ned Kelly went to the gallows on 11 November 1880.

After death, a mask was made of his head and was then decapitated and the skull boiled. Kelly was a stoic to the last: 'It's no use blaming anyone now,' he said at his trial. 'It is not that I fear death. I fear it as little as to drink a cup of tea. On the evidence that has been given, no juryman could have given any other verdict. That is my opinion. But, as I say, if I'd examined the witnesses, I'd had shown matters in a different light … For my own part, I don't care one straw about my life, nor the result of the trial; and I know very well from the stories I've been told, of how I am spoken of- that the public at large execrate my name … But I don't mind, for I am the last that carries public favour or dreads the public frown. Let the hand of the law strike me down if it will; but I ask my story be heard and considered.'

His final words were said to be, 'Such Is Life'

ACKNOWLEDGEMENTS

The following people made this book possible; Jody Lee who edited the manuscript under great pressure; Rose Creswell, Lesley McFadzean and Sophie Hamley at Cameron's Management, Stuart Neal at ABC Books who commissioned it over Chinese, Chris Hogg who inspired it over a beer. There have been too many supporters to acknowledge all of them but John O'Donnell, Clinton Walker, Martin Fabinyi, John Bush, Jolyon Burnett, Tara Anderson, Peter Doyle and Catherine Courtenay deserve thanks. Finally, my family who have put up with it; the Trenoweths, Timothy Singleton, Michael Creswell and, most of all, Samantha Trenoweth and Alice Trenoweth-Creswell.

www.ingramcontent.com/pod-product-compliance
Lightning Source LLC
Chambersburg PA
CBHW022042290426
44109CB00014B/950